IT NEVER RAINS UNLESS IT TO

THE FASCINATING – AND OFTEN TEMPESTUOUS –
LIFE OF ONE OF BRITAIN'S FOREMOST
TV COMMERCIAL PRODUCERS.

Geoffrey Forster

Foreword by Petula Clark

Acknowledgements

Producer: Tom Leppard
Editor: Shane Harrison
Consultant: D. Richard Truman
Technical Advisor: Sarah Leppard
Cover Design: Shamus Smith

**Grosvenor House
Publishing Limited**

This book is published by
Grosvenor House Publishing Ltd
Link House
140 The Broadway, Tolworth, Surrey, KT6 7HT.
www.grosvenorhousepublishing.co.uk

A CIP record for this book
is available from the British Library

ISBN 978-1-83975-267-4

Dedication

This book is affectionately dedicated to
my children Sarah, Jane and Jonathan.
And to my grandchildren
Matthew, Ben, Tom, Sophie, Florence,
Henry, and Esme,
who have given me so much pleasure over the years.

And to my wife, Shirley, who has put up with me for
over sixty years,
and whose comment when she heard I was writing this
book was:

"I suppose you are going to become a bloody bore
about that, now."

Such is love.

Foreword

cher Geoff,

Wow! Has it really been 40-plus years since we worked on the Chrysler Sunbeam commercial together? When was it? 1977? I think so. Where did all the years go? But you know, I can still remember it as though it was yesterday! Like the time you and Richard Lester, the director, met me at the Hôtel Plaza Athénée in Paris to hammer out some of the finer details. And then, of course, there was the shoot itself. We left London in a fleet of limos and luxury buses, and a huge truck with an extra Sunbeam car – just in case! I remember thinking to myself, all this for one little television ad? And don't forget the Sunbeam song the agency came up with. It wasn't bad at all. The shoot was great fun, too. More like a slightly mad holiday than proper work.

Amicalement,

Petula Clark

Setting The Scene

During my fifty years as a producer of commercials in the advertising business, I always had good weather or, if I needed bad weather to trigger an insurance claim, I got it. As a result, I never lost a single penny due to inclement weather. And that is the reason behind the title of this book, *It Never Rains Unless I Want It To©*. Enjoy.

Author's Note

There are no individual chapters per se in this book, rather a series of sections covering the different stages of my life and business career.

And while some dates may be mentioned, no attempt has been made to structure them into anything resembling strict chronological order.

Table Of Contents

1. RELATIVE VALUES   1
2. CAREER CHOICES   21
3. THE NEW MEDIUM   37
4. COMMERCIAL BREAKS   45
5. SETTING RECORDS   57
6. PRINCIPLES MATTER   69
7. ON MY OWN   91
8. PRODUCING RESULTS   167
9. SPOT OF RAIN   279

1

RELATIVE VALUES

I first started writing this humble effort – modesty precludes me from calling it a *memoir* – as I approached my 75th birthday. Now, in my 87th year, it is at long last in the rear view mirror. Put to bed, as they say. Done and most definitely dusted. Every last 'i' dotted, every single 't' crossed. So what motivated this old codger to undertake a task of such Herculean magnitude? Was it, as some have suggested, a vainglorious attempt at immortality? Or maybe it was simply the desire to give readers an insight into the varied – and often turbulent – life I have led, warts and all?

The seed, I vividly recall, was sown a few years back when our eldest daughter mentioned she might like to open a shop. I looked at her askance. You see I once had occasion to "manage" a shop myself. A bookshop, to be precise. (Let's just say it wasn't my finest hour.) "I never knew you ran a shop, dad," she said, making no attempt to conceal the amazement in her voice.

At that precise moment, it occurred to me that my own children – my kith and kin – knew very little about their father, his life and career. So this book is affectionately dedicated to them, as well as to my seven wonderful grandchildren, and indeed, all future Forster generations.

In 2007, our younger daughter and her partner decamped the UK for Australia with four of our grandchildren in tow, and now have Australian citizenship. When I mentioned to her I was writing this book, she said with an ever-so-slightly sardonic smirk, "Well you had better hurry up with it so that I can read it from the pulpit." Such comments pass for humour in our family.

As was seemingly common in many Victorian and Edwardian families, my father never once – that I am able to recall – mentioned his childhood or his parents, both of them had passed away before I was born. What I have since learned about my grandparents has been assiduously gleaned from old photographs, personal childhood memories, notes my mother and maternal grandmother kept, and, quite literally, weeks and weeks of online research.

The Forster family home in the 1920s and 1930s was a rather modest semi-detached Victorian house on Trewsbury Road, Sydenham in South East London. I remember it well, with its weather-beaten conservatory almost completely overgrown with some nameless, yet prolific, creeper. The garden was pleasant, consisting of a lawn surrounded by a gravel path with rose arches at regular intervals. I particularly remember the family dog, an Airedale called Monty. I still have a photograph of myself, aged about three, with Monty in that garden.

My grandparents had eight children, three of whom died very young. Millicent and Helen didn't survive infancy, while William died when he was sixteen. My father would have been four years of age when this happened, which may at least partially explain his reticence to discuss the family.

There were two older brothers and two sisters, my father being the youngest sibling. He was born in 1904, though his death certificate erroneously states 1903. (A slip-up on my brother's part when he registered the death.) The two brothers were named Guy and Herbert and the sisters, Nellie and Marion. My father was christened Archibald. Grandfather Forster was a reader for the *Morning Times*, which must have been quite a responsible job. His father had been a compositor, presumably with the same newspaper.

My earliest memory of the house was the Christmas we spent there in, I think, 1937. Despite the obvious passage of time, in my mind's eye I can still clearly see every detail of every room, including the scullery, and even the cellar where the coal was stored.

The part of the house our family occupied that Christmas was situated high up in the attic. It could only be reached by climbing a long and perilous staircase that struck terror into me – I was going to be four in a couple of months – when I had to pass it on the way to the bathroom, situated half way up the house on the middle floor. (Since then, visiting the WC in the Forster household has always been referred to as going "half way".)

Uncle Herbert was in the meteorological service of the Royal Air Force. While Uncle Guy worked all his life for the Commercial Union insurance company. And, by all accounts, absolutely loathed it. He stuck it out, however, and our son is now the proud custodian of the gold watch presented to him on his retirement. He was a tremendously talented man who installed the first electric lighting in the house.

Aunt Nellie, who never married, worked as a Civil Servant and eventually lived in a flat in Du Cane Court between Clapham and Streatham. Aunt Marion also remained a spinster and was in the retail trade, quite possibly a cashier in Dickens and Jones, a department store in Regent Street. Her death certificate lists her as an accounts clerk. She lived in a flat on Clapham Common and later moved to Hastings.

Both Guy and Herbert were immensely gifted craftsmen. I first learned of Herbert's redoubtable talent from his stepson when my wife and I attended the funeral of my cousin, his only daughter, Aline. I have in my possession a walking stick Herbert fashioned from a section of a propeller that was given to my father by his brother. It is a truly magnificent piece of work.

Guy eventually built his own garage in Sanderstead, and fitted the kitchen with built-in cupboards long before such things were readily available in DIY stores. He also created practical objects made from iron, including a number of light fittings, one of which I have to this day.

Sadly, the creative genes my two uncles possessed were not shared with my father. To his credit, however, he was particularly adept at crochet work. And I can imagine he may well have been pondering one of his challenging algebraic puzzles as he wielded the crochet hook. My wife and I still have a beautiful tablecloth that undoubtedly took him many hours to complete. He started work with an insurance company, a decision possibly influenced by his older brother, Guy. He then transferred to the Stock Exchange. But, being rather deaf, found it difficult to survive the rough and tumble of the trading floor.

As Herbert had only the one daughter and Guy no children, the responsibility for carrying on the family line fell to my father. I was born on 10 January, 1934, and my sister Gillian on 5 February, 1938. My younger brother, Christopher, was born six years later on 13 April, 1944.

My parents were married in July 1929. My mother, who did not get on with her own mother, had left home and was living with her aunt on Leonard Road in Sydenham.

Mother and father were both keen tennis players in their youth. In fact, it is quite possible they first met at the tennis club situated halfway between their two houses. Yet, despite their shared interest in tennis, I doubt they had much else in common. My mother had studied piano, and had taken singing lessons, but she never had a career. She was just twenty-one when she married and had probably met my father when she was in her late teens.

Educated at Wilson's Grammar School in South London, my father clearly had a very good brain, but lacked the practical skills of his two older brothers.

After his less than successful stint at the Stock Exchange, his sister Nellie got him a job in the Civil Service. He joined the Ministry of Supply and thus had a reserved occupation when war broke out in 1939. Due to his occupation, we got our first telephone, a shared line with the number Orpington 4541. As he didn't manage to pass the Civil Service exam – the most common way to gain entry into the Service in those days – he would remain a "temporary" Civil Servant. This would have far-reaching consequences later in his career.

Shortly after they married, my parents bought a small three-bedroom house in Orpington for the princely sum of £800. It was detached with a good-sized garden. In those far off days, sheep still grazed almost all the way down to the war memorial at the junction of Spur Road and the high street.

I was born in a private nursing home in Lawrie Park Road, Sydenham and was a little reluctant to arrive, or so I am told. I am fairly sure my sister was also born there. I was absent for that event as I had been banished to stay with my maternal grandmother in her flat in Colyton Road, East Dulwich.

During my exile to my one and only grandmother, I remember being taken to visit a tool shop in Vauxhall, which I now realise was a pawnbroker run by one of her relatives. I have never forgotten being shown a large hand drill – known as a "Belly Buster" – and afterwards standing on Vauxhall Bridge looking down on the tugboats lowering their funnels as they passed beneath me.

My grandmother, Annie Elizabeth Johnson, had lived with her husband in Gowlet Road, East Dulwich. This was where my mother and her older sister, Elsie, along with their brother, Maurice, were brought up. My grandfather died in his forties and with three children to bring up, life must have been pretty grim. Grandma took in lodgers to help make ends meet. It has been suggested that perhaps one or two guests got more than board and lodging. There is no hard evidence to corroborate this unless you take into account the fact that the first child, Elsie, was born rather soon after the wedding!

I do not know exactly when she moved into her flat, but the youngest child, my uncle Maurice, was still living with her. The flat overlooked Peckham Rye Park – a veritable wonderland to a small boy. There were ducks to feed and many small streams and ponds to splosh about in. It was most heartening to discover recently that it had been refurbished with the aid of a Millennium Commission grant, with nearly all the original features retained.

At the time, Orpington was a rapidly expanding area just south east of London. My father christened our house, The Gambit, which is an opening move in the game of chess. Chess was something he clearly enjoyed, and he was quite a skilled player.

The Orpington high street always held a great fascination for me as a young boy. There was the blacksmith shoeing horses owned by local farmers and tradesmen, the Commodore cinema, Sparrows the tobacconist, a very popular bakery and a little further on Edwards, the boot and shoe repairer.

Also located along this particular stretch was what must have been one of the first Tesco shops. It was open fronted and had shutters that were pulled down at night. The Tesco name first appeared in 1924 when a market trader by the name of Jack Cohen bought a large shipment of tea and rebranded it using the first three letters of the company he ordered it from, T.E. Stockwell, followed by the first two letters of his surname. Hence T.E.S.C.O.

At the far end of the street was a small turning housing the village hall where we all went to have our wartime gas masks fitted. Then there was a turning to the priory and the parish church where I was baptised in April 1934. Finally there was the village pond and the timber yard where, many years later, I would be able to buy bundles of offcuts to feed my growing passion for carpentry.

On the opposite side of the high street was a café, Lewis's the tobacconist, newsagent and sweet shop, and Lanes the stationers where I used to buy passé-partout, a tough coloured paper strip with a gummed back I used to frame postcards with the small panes of glass that were blown out of our leaded windows by the Doodlebugs.

A little further along was Cave Austin, a rather upmarket grocer where we bought our rations during the war. I remember the large slabs of butter and cheese from which our meagre allowance was cut, and the rows of biscuit tins temptingly angled towards the customers.

Woolworths, in those days still a threepenny and sixpenny store, was an Aladdin's cave and destined to be the source of many of my purchases as I grew up. Another shop I fondly recall was Stapley, where I bought my first-ever tool. It was a carpenter's brace for which I parted with the astronomical sum of fourteen shillings and sixpence!

Local deliverymen were constant visitors to our house. The milkman every day, the greengrocer twice a week, and every so often the rag-and-bone man with his horse and cart would drop by, as would the children's ultimate favourite, the Walls ice cream tricycle.

The family house itself was on Lancing Road, at the base of a hill. This meant that there was a slight slope in the garden from left to right as you stood with your back to the rear of the house. This was where father added a conservatory featuring large panes of glass criss-crossed with lead strips to give the impression of separate panes. The adhesive holding the strips in place gave up the ghost after a while, and the lead fell off and became a rather welcome distraction for a small boy wanting to make things.

The school I attended was called Montclair House, where the boys sported pink blazers and, in summer, the girls wore cream-coloured shantung silk dresses. I remember only one girl at school, Susan Walker. She sticks out in my mind because once when we were singing the traditional song, "Linden Lea", in music class, both of us got a fit of the giggles when it came to the line "... and waters bubbling in its bed."

When war was declared, Mother, Gill and I slept under the stairs for the first month or two. I remember the pair of us sitting on the top step leading to our back door watching the Battle of Britain. On the horizon was a railway embankment and beyond that Biggin Hill, so we had a grandstand view. After some time, presumably when the Blitz was at its height, Mother, Gill and I were sent to Westbury in Wiltshire. Westbury Liegh was the home of the Kitley family and the birthplace of my great grandfather.

As a child I do not remember being terrified at any stage during the war. Sometimes at night my sister and I would be in a double bed and made a make-believe gun emplacement from pillows and a bolster as actual anti-aircraft guns echoed in the night sky above us. In the morning we would search the floor for shrapnel or the silver foil the German bombers dropped to confuse the radar.

Some of our friends had air raid shelters. Either the man of the house would dig his own or they bought an Anderson which was made of corrugated iron and buried into the ground at least halfway and the top covered with earth. We eventually got a Morrison shelter that was basically a steel cage that sat where our dining table once was. With heavy steel corners and a sheet steel top and grills, you could attach the front, back and sides so you would feel completely safe inside.

Living next door to us were three elderly ladies, a Mrs. Goffin, a Miss Frost and one whose name escapes me. They had connections with a well-off Catholic family and I suspect that one of the ladies was a relative of Mr. Wetz, who arranged for a heavy concrete shelter to be built onto the side of their house. Mrs. Goffin seemed to be in charge and she was a very welcome source of pocket money. I used to dig up the chicken run and tidy the garden and was usually given five shillings – sometimes as much as seven shillings and sixpence – a veritable fortune to me at eight or nine.

It must have been as a result of visiting other houses and seeing their elaborate shelters, that encouraged me to dig my own. By the end of the war, I had dug out a shelter at the bottom of our garden with the aid of the boy next door, Brian Skinner. We got a lot of materials from local bombsites and built a shelter large enough for the two of us, with a bunk across one end, a door in from the path and an escape hatch concealed by a dustbin lid cover. With bricks from demolished houses and other items including a large sheet of lead, we built a fireplace and, on occasion, flames could be seen coming from the mud and brick chimney. No such things as Health and Safety in those days, and of course building materials were everywhere just begging to be picked up.

This was almost certainly when my love of building and the desire to become an architect was born.

My father was in the Air Raid Precautions (ARP) and would sometimes be out on the streets searching for stray lights in the blackout. On other occasions he would be on duty all night in the headquarters that were in an undeveloped area known as The Walnuts. I remember being allowed to join him there one night. I wanted to become a Boy Scout, but when I asked if I could join the Cubs, mother put her foot down. The meeting place was in the recreation ground that housed a searchlight and anti-aircraft battery, so it was completely out of the question as far as she was concerned.

As the war progressed and air raids became a nightly occurrence, Gillian and I were sent to stay with our Aunt Ruby in York. I instantly fell in love with the city and used to enjoy walking the ancient walls. After some time, mother joined us and we relocated to an area near the River Foss. I will never forget climbing to the top of York Minster and being terrified of falling through the stone tracery of the surrounding parapet. We did not stay very long in York and returned to Orpington just as the flying bombs started to rain down on British cities.

'V-1 flying bombs, or Doodlebugs as they were called, landed indiscriminately and you would listen out for the deep, throaty noise of the engine and when it cut out wait for the inevitable explosion. Several of them landed fairly close to us but, mercifully, we suffered only minor damage. I remember one event in particular when I heard the familiar engine noise cut out and rushed into the garden to where my baby brother was in his pram. It was a close call and my brother was lucky to escape with no more than a slight scratch on his forehead. Most of our windows were blown out and, as they were leaded, gave me more useful lead and lots of small panes of glass to play with. Our windows were repaired with Windolite™, a sort of translucent plastic on a wire mesh.

There was a silver lining to this otherwise dark cloud as I learned valuable lessons from watching the workmen who were sent to repair our splintered door and window frames. How to splice a new section into damaged wood is a skill that is still with me today.

While we are on the subject of lead, it seems my obsession with this highly practical and malleable metal may have been the cause of the persistent stomach problems I was beset with, both as a child and later in adulthood. I frequently suffered from loss of appetite, abdominal cramps and vomiting. The cause of which continued to confound our local doctor. Some ten years ago, I watched a documentary on lead poisoning and there were all my childhood symptoms. In the thirties and forties the dangers were just not known as water had been delivered to homes through lead pipes for generations.

Television in England had been shut down the moment Germany invaded Poland in 1939. So the radio became our main source of information, entertainment and companionship. We used to listen to the news, often read by Frank Phillips, Alvar Lidell or John Snagge, all of whom I would meet later in my working life. Some of my earliest memories are of *Children's Hour with Uncle Mac,* which included my two favourite programmes, *Toy Town* and *Romany with Raq.* I also well remember *Worker's Playtime, Music While You Work* and entertainment programmes such as *Hippodrome* and *Itma* with Tommy Handley, which, incidentally, I was not supposed to listen to as father did not approve.

13

During the war years, even people of modest means had help in the house. For many years mother had Mrs. Cronin, whose husband worked for the railway as a ticket collector at Orpington Station. He had had an accident at some stage and lost one of his arms. Mrs. Cronin became part of the family and was difficult to replace when she eventually left. Her replacement was a woman I did not take to at all. To make matters worse, I discovered that she had almost certainly stolen some of my lead farm animals. When we visited her once for tea in her bungalow on Court Road, I was amazed to see them displayed on the mantelpiece in her sitting room!

We knew most of our neighbours, and often mixed with them socially. It was nothing at all like today when people tend to remain at home behind closed doors, watching television or playing on their computers or Smartphones. There were the Windles, Taylors, Stevens, Leggets, Rossiters, Skinners, Boehms, Neerys, Chaplins, Blackburns, and of course Mrs. Goffin, and her two friends next door.

At the age of eleven, I passed the entrance exam to Dulwich College Preparatory School. To this day, I have three abiding memories of my time there. Namely school lunches, studying Latin, and my very first carpentry lessons.

The school lunches gave me a lasting aversion to roast meals. I initially found Latin difficult to master. I was even bottom of the class one term. But the very next term, under the tutelage of the deputy headmaster,

I came top and still have the form prize to prove it. It taught me the valuable lesson: do not always blame the child.

My third memory revolves around taking carpentry lessons at lunchtime from a retired army officer, Captain Fleming. He taught me how to sharpen my tools and make a mortise and tenon joint. With this newly acquired knowledge I made mother an egg rack, while I received a lasting passion for woodworking.

Having started making things at age nine or ten, one birthday I was given a small tenon saw and, at some stage, received a wooden vice that could be clamped onto the kitchen table. The first foray into carpentry was a toboggan made out of wood claimed from a bombsite. It was far too heavy and I learned the hard way that you cannot make toboggan runners out of lead. I very quickly made three lightweight sledges with steel runners. They were painted in different colours, mine were white, my sister's red and my brother's blue. I soon became a regular visitor to the timber yard carrying my bunch of offcuts over my shoulder all the way back up the high street.

I made my mother a cream-painted medicine box with a red cross on top. I also started to make table lamps with small photo frames set into the base using little panes of glass from our broken windows. I once made a lamp with an ashtray in the base for my father. All the lamps were made of oak and I was greatly helped by our next door but one neighbour, Mr. Taylor, who taught me how to finish and French polish.

When the war in Europe ended in May 1945, there were celebrations everywhere. The neighbours got together to make a huge bonfire using the blackout material and black felt that had covered many of our windows during air raids. Our road was selected to host the celebration. Hopes were high as the bonfire was duly lit, but one resident, a Mr. Legget, called the police and complained that the flames were blistering the paint on his front door. We all thought that highly unlikely and the police agreed. There is always one.

Not long after, we were on the move again, this time to Beckenham. My father purchased a semi-detached house at 65 Whitmore Road. It had four bedrooms and a garage that was to become my very first workshop. The move was clearly instigated by my mother as the house was opposite that of her cousin who she had become very close to when she had moved in with her Aunt Emily.

By now I had passed into Dulwich College. The shorter train journey to school and my new garage workshop combined to keep me very happy. One birthday I was given a copy of *Charles Hayward's Carpentry Book*. From it I was able to make my small brother a desk and chair. I also made a television table for our next-door neighbours, Mr. and Mrs. Chappay. My most enjoyable project involved making a dolls house – based on my own design – with a fully functioning electric light in every room.

Although we were by no means a wealthy family, we always seemed to manage an annual holiday. Once during the war we stayed on a farm near Coombe Martin in Devon. I well remember the farmer's wife making Devon cream on an enormous kitchen range. We had a long daily walk down to the sea and on one occasion I went fishing with my father. I caught nothing, but have always wondered if the small tug I felt on the line just might have been supper.

Before the war, we had holidayed in Paignton, a pretty seaside town in Devon. We went there twice more after 1945 when I was twelve and thirteen. The host family where we were staying had two daughters about my age, and I think I may have been the cause of some friction between them on our second visit. The first time we stayed with them, one of the sisters clearly wanted to be my friend. However in year two, it was the other one who took a shine to me, which caused some upset between the two girls.

Although I was not unpopular, I really had only one close friend at school. Alan Burgess and I were literally inseparable during these years. One of our regular pursuits was playing tennis on the courts of the sports ground almost opposite Alan's house. The courts were private and owned by a company, Barclay Perkins. On the afternoon of 25 April, 1950, we enjoyed a hotly contested match. When our time was up, a couple schoolgirls, who were next on court, got talking to us. I must have summoned up an extra ounce of courage that day because I was really quite shy, and certainly would not have chatted to them on my own.

There was snow piled at the side of the court and it was quite cold, but by the time we left them we must have agreed to meet them again, or at least found out where they went to school and the route they took home. We did meet them again and discovered they were going on holiday together to a holiday camp called New Beach at East Wittering on the South Coast near Chichester. Unbeknownst to them, Alan and I booked into the same camp – at the same time – and gave them quite a surprise, I can tell you.

The two girls in question were Shirley Hammerton and Jean Barnes. I have no idea whether they were pleased or upset to see us there. Not wanting Shirley to get into trouble, I immediately wrote to her father to explain the situation. To make a long story short, six years later I married Shirley while her friend, Jean, was one of her bridesmaids.

I was not very happy attending school six days a week as it gave me very little free time to pursue my main hobby of carpentry. By now I was working on more elaborate projects, including a bathroom stool with an inset cork top, and a kitchen cupboard. It would not be long before I was making furniture and by the time Shirley and I were married, I had produced a coffee table, record cabinet and a chest of drawers, all in oak, as well as an oak chest stained with creosote to give it an antique appearance. This particular piece, by the way, is still owned by our son. I also had a part-time job working for the local tool and timber shop, a sort of mini-DIY shop. I made many shelves, storage boxes and other fittings for the shop, some of which I made at home due to my compulsory sport on Saturday afternoons.

I recently discovered that, after many years, my fittings were still in situ.

I took the School Certificate examinations – the forerunner of O Levels – and did well in some subjects, but not well enough to reach the standard needed to gain my matriculation. I was sent to a crammer in Holland Park, Kensington – Davies, Laing and Dick (DLD) – and sat a few other subjects the following year. The results were distinctions in mathematics, general science and technical drawing, along with credits in English, French and a couple of other subjects. It was precisely what I needed to pursue my chosen career as an architect.

A child can be very sensitive and I was acutely aware on Founder's Day each June that my parents came to the school by train, while most other parents arrived in Bentleys or Jaguars. I do, however, remember my mother wearing her first "New Look" featuring a blue and white floral pattern.

There was not much affection shown in our family, my father being rather Victorian, and mother certainly incapable of showing affection of any kind.

Unfortunately mother became rather unstable during the latter part of the 1940s and I know that after the birth of my brother there were consultations with the doctor that today would probably be called psychiatric counselling. At one time all the sharp knives in the house had to be hidden. It must have had some effect on me as I had to attend the doctor and was told that I needed to get away from home. My mother's reaction was instant and she threatened to commit suicide if I did leave. It was not a happy situation.

In the election of 1951, Churchill was returned to power. The immediate fallout from this was a greater demand for economies and a reduction of the Civil Service. My father, being a "temporary" Civil Servant, faced the very real prospect of losing his job. With three children at school, he had to accept a permanency – but at half his previous salary! My sister had won a scholarship to the local grammar school so she was safe, but it was to be the end of school for me. The fees were simply unaffordable. Being ten years younger, my brother was sent to a private Catholic school.

Another side effect of my father's misfortune was the family was forced to move yet again, this time to an end of terrace house in The Drive, Beckenham, which ran between the high street and the station. Today we call it downsizing, but it must have been a bitter pill for my father to swallow at the time.

So there I was, aged seventeen, my education unfinished, and having to find gainful employment. But, as luck would have it, one of our neighbours was a partner in a small recording studio in London, and he was looking for a junior.

2

CAREER CHOICES

On a bright summer morning in 1951, I started work at United Motion Pictures (UMP) of 24 Denmark Street, close to London's West End. My salary as a projectionist and general dogsbody was a paltry three pounds and ten shillings a week. I don't know how much that figure would be worth in today's money. Let's just say not a lot. My main function was to project images from 16mm film onto a translucent screen enabling voiceover artists, situated in a soundproof booth, to add their dulcet tones to various industrial or medical films.

One of our larger clients at the time, Imperial Chemical Industries, or ICI, had their own film unit based in Billingham and produced a monthly newsletter. Each month two clients from the company would arrive in London to finalise the newsreels they had just shot. The commentators I met working on these productions included the likes of John Snagge, Frank Phillips, Alvar Lidell and others who were regular newsreaders on the BBC. Once the recording was over, they would adjourn to a Soho restaurant to enjoy a good dinner. But, alas, not the poor projectionist, I'm afraid!

In those days, before the advent of magnetic tape as a recording medium, the recording was done straight onto film. If a mistake was made, the recording was immediately stopped and an overlap put in place so that the resulting strip of film could be edited.

By this time Shirley and I were what today is often referred to as an item. She had left school and enrolled in Beckenham Art College. She no doubt blames our relationship for not completing her course. I have always considered this a very great pity as she had – and, quite honestly, still does have – not inconsiderable talent. We also became fairly regular concertgoers at the Albert Hall at a cost of two shillings and sixpence a concert.

In April 1952, I received my call-up for National Service. I joined the Queen's Own Royal West Kent Regiment at their barracks in Maidstone, spent a lot of time in Canterbury and was eventually commissioned in the East Surrey Regiment and sent to Egypt. Overall, this experience was really quite enjoyable. It also taught me some invaluable life lessons.

When I boarded the train at Beckenham Junction station on my way to join up, I met another conscript, who had got on at the previous station. His name was Graham Pedgrift. After our initial six weeks of training, both Graham and I were put forward for officer training and became officer cadets at the Buffs Barracks in Canterbury.

Overnight exercises took place either on the training area next to the barracks or the cliffs above Dover. During my last trip to the latter, I committed the cardinal sin of falling asleep and had my rifle taken by the opposition.

I don't recall the exact punishment, but it was not terribly serious. While on the cliffs, I came across an entrance on the cliff wall leading to a flight of steps heading down into the cliffs. I ventured down but did not explore any further. In 2015, I was very surprised to learn that the National Trust had opened the very spot to the public.

At the end of the course we faced a practical test held at a training establishment in Wiltshire. It was known as WOSB, or War Office Selection Board. I duly took the test, but did not pass and so returned to Canterbury as a lance corporal. I would, however, have the opportunity to retake the test in three months' time. Very unusually for me this happened twice. I was probably regarded as being too shy, but, in truth, I would not talk for talking's sake – only when I had a worthwhile contribution to make to the conversation.

During my time in Canterbury as a lance corporal, I soon discovered that if I walked out of the barracks looking as though I was on a mission, I was never questioned and could walk across the training area to the nearest village. I was no longer in the Buffs Barracks, rather the old cavalry barracks at the bottom of the hill. The Cathedral was my favourite place to visit and there were many other historical sites in the town. Occasionally there was a church parade when the sergeant in command would shout for us to fall in using the expression, "Arsees, parsees, and buckshees!"

Having unfortunately missed my confirmation at school due to a dose of chicken pox, I decided that I should now be confirmed, so I took the requisite classes with our resident padre and was confirmed by the Bishop of Dover in Canterbury Cathedral. My parents attended along with my godfather, Denis Writer, an old family friend who presented me with a set of gold cufflinks.

There's an old army saying, "Bullshit baffles brains". Basically it means that if you can manage to impress, or distract, people with trifling details, they may miss the bigger picture. My uncanny ability to shine my boots until I could see my face in them served me well as I was seldom inspected and went on to win two medals as best cadet and best shot. I spent nearly a year in Canterbury and got to know it very well. But I found myself missing Shirley terribly, and took every opportunity to get back to see her at weekends.

On my third attempt at the selection process, I passed and was sent for officer training at Eaton Hall in Cheshire. During my training I was, on more than one occasion, excused from parade and given a camera with instructions to record the event for posterity.

Chester is a very old town and although we did not have many opportunities to visit it, I will always remember walking the old walls just as I had done in York. During my time there, the May Ball took place and Shirley was able to visit me, staying in Blossoms Hotel in the town. For my passing out parade and commissioning, my parents came up, and booked a room in a village just outside the estate.

When I was finally commissioned, I had too little time left to be able to join the West Kent Battalion that was serving in Malaya. So I was given a commission in the East Surrey Regiment based in Kingston and was sent to join the battalion in Egypt.

This was quite possibly a very lucky escape as Malaya in 1953 was not a good place to be. My journey to join my new battalion at Tel El Kebir in the Canal Zone was to take a week and it marked the first time I had been further than the Isle of Wight.

As an officer I was (quite rightly, I hasten to add) entitled to travel first class. Our train set out from Liverpool Street to Harwich on the East Coast, where we boarded a small ship, the *Empire Wambeck*. We were then transported to the Hook of Holland where we caught another train that was to take thirty-six hours to reach our destination of Trieste. As I had a first class sleeping compartment, I enjoyed a very pleasant – and restful – journey through beautiful scenery. Upon our arrival, we embarked on another ship, this time the *Empire Ken*, for a four-day cruise on the Mediterranean to the city of Port Said, in north east Egypt. The (mercifully) final leg of our journey saw us travel by train along the canal to our destination where I was met by a truck, clearly steerage class!

I cannot recall whether it was on my first or second evening in Port Said that I was asked to join in a card game by my new brother officers. The game was whist and I remember one of the players was the quartermaster. How it came about I do not know, but that evening I won and was never asked to join them again! Nearly all National Service second lieutenants became infantry platoon commanders, the most junior of officers.

For some unknown reason I was given charge of an anti-tank platoon. This meant I was responsible for a much larger group of men and much more equipment, some of which was new and on desert trials. It also meant that I had my own batman and Champ – an English version of a Jeep – and travelled with the commanding officer when on the road.

While in Egypt I was taken by my company commander to visit some old friends of his in the Paras. We went swimming at the Officer's Club in Moascar and generally had a pretty good time. On various exercises I learned many lessons that would be of great use to me in the future. Writing part one and part two orders made doing a call sheet for a day's filming quite a simple matter. There was a brigade support company competition during my time and I was able to win it. But I did not always get things right!

We had new Humber trucks on desert trials and they were used to tow the new recoilless anti-tank guns that, along with Stuart tanks and 17-pounder anti-tank guns, were part of my platoon.

The Humbers were very prone to breaking down and oil seals were always going. On one exercise, I lost two of my convoy and made the basic mistake of setting off from our evening camp to find them. The inevitable happened and I, along with my batman driver, got stuck in a salt marsh and when we eventually got back to camp, the missing vehicles were both there.

I must have been given a severe telling off by my company commander, but a very important lesson had been learned.

There was one other incident that occurred when towing a 17-pounder anti-tank gun to a Royal Electrical and Mechanical Engineers (R.E.M.E) workshop for some minor maintenance. I was, to say the least, surprised when one of the wheels of the gun sheared off and overtook us. I was fully expecting a court martial, but nothing was ever said. Perhaps the worst thing that ever happened to me was not my fault at all. I have always had the ability to sleep soundly, whether outside under a lorry or in bed after a two- or three-day exercise. After one such event I slept for more than twenty-four hours, missing one complete day. I eventually got up and went into the mess for breakfast only to hear a buzz of conversation about the fire. "What fire?" I asked and was told to cross the parade ground to look at my own platoon lines. I did so and to my horror discovered that there were no tents left, only charred cupboards and bedsteads.

I was up in front of the commanding officer that morning, but I simply had not heard the bugler sounding the alarm, so not much could be done. Two days later another alarm sounded in the officers' quarters and, fortunately, someone made sure I heard it.

We would occasionally venture outside our mined perimeter and on one such occasion I was standing in one of my Stuart carriers. It was not until the commanding officer shouted at me that I realised I was being shot at. Luckily for me he was not much of a shot and missed. Another shooting incident was very much worse and happened when we were on guard duty at a wartime ammunition dump.

Two of my men were patrolling together at night and both were carrying Sten guns. One of the soldiers had a hole in his army issue sweater and as he hitched up his Sten, which was slung over his shoulder, the cocking lever caught in the hole and he accidentally shot his mate who was to tragically die in my arms. It was clearly an accident, and I do not remember any serious punishment to the soldier concerned.

What I do remember is sitting down to write a letter that I hope never to have to write again. It was to the mother of the dead man. It was especially upsetting as she was a widow and an invalid, and her son was soon due to be given a compassionate discharge to look after her. Life can deal some very harsh blows.

About a month before I was due to be demobbed, I was duty officer when a sergeant, who was one of my own platoon, started to cause trouble. It was clearly a matter of drink, but I had to discipline him and put him on a charge that was quite serious. In the mess I was told that he would face a court martial and that as I would be a key witness, which meant my departure back to the UK would be delayed.

Luckily, I was released back to the UK on time, and flew back in a Dakota via Malta.

To this day I do not know what had singled me out for special treatment, but perhaps my seniors saw something in me that I was unaware of at the time. If I may quote the testimonial I received when I left the army, it perhaps indicates that I had used my time well in preparation for my future career.

"A very cheerful young National Service officer who would be a great asset to the battalion if his civilian occupation permitted him to volunteer. He commanded the anti-tank platoon very efficiently during annual training. He has self-confidence and is quick to overcome difficulties and take responsibility."

I was offered a place at Sandhurst if I was willing to sign on for a further year, but being aware that I would not be able to marry without my commanding officer's permission, it was a no-brainer. Soon after my demob, I proposed to Shirley, although not in very romantic circumstances. To celebrate, I took her to Covent Garden to see a performance of *La Traviata*.

I returned to work at United Motion Pictures – a rather grand name for an insignificant little company – and was immediately made manager on the huge salary of eight pounds a week! Working in such a small company had many advantages that were to stand me in good stead in the years to come.

Although most of our work was on 16mm film, I was to get my first experience of working with 35mm when we made a cinema appeal for St. Dunstan's, the home and training centre for blind servicemen on the outskirts of Brighton. I was the assistant to Forbes Taylor, a freelance director, who had a previous association with the company. As there were only two of us on the shoot, being his assistant meant loading the camera, keeping focus and doing all the carrying around that normally would be done by a camera grip.

We stayed at the White Horse Hotel in Rottingdean and filmed for a couple of days and I recall many of the scenes we covered. How to light a cigarette with the match held on the end, how to pour a drink with one finger over the top of the glass and how to recognise coins by size and their milled edge.

On that occasion I had to work with a Debrie camera that took a 1000-foot reel of 35mm film and must have been the heaviest camera ever made; it had to be supported on a Vinten heavy-duty tripod that was almost as big as I was.

Later I worked on a documentary that Forbes made on the life of an aspiring actress and, as it so happens, his future wife. We filmed in theatres, the Royal Academy of Dramatic Art and the offices of Equity, the actors union. What happened to the film I do not know or whether the lady had any success in her chosen career.

Forbes Taylor was later to offer me another job that could, potentially, have lead almost anywhere within the ITV network. He was offering me the job as Head of Films for Anglia. But the move to Norwich was quickly

– and understandably – vetoed by Shirley who had an invalid mother living on the south coast.

As time went on, the company took on various small industrial productions of its own and I was able to graduate from backroom boy to editor, writer, director and cameraman. I also became an associate member of the Institute of British Photographers and the British Kinematograph Society (BKS).

I attended a lecture on densitometry and sensitometry given by the BKS and, although not meaning too much to me at the time, I have never forgotten it. It gave me a basic understanding of the problems that television would have, especially with the imminent advent of colour.

As an editor, I had many interesting projects and could frequently be found sitting in a small room with a projector at my side showing a scene on the wall about five feet away. Magnetic tape had just been invented and a magnetic stripe could be put on the soundtrack area of 16mm film enabling one to add sound effects from a tape recorder to synchronise with the action on screen. It was quite skilled and a marvellous learning.

On several occasions I worked with Lord Wakehurst, who I discovered subsequently was a former governor of New South Wales and of Northern Ireland. Though, obviously, not at the same time.

He was a trustee of the Royal Opera House and a governor of the Royal Ballet and frequently stood in the wings at Covent Garden shooting silent 16mm film. It became my task to try and make sense of the disconnected footage and to work with the Royal Ballet Company's rehearsal pianist who had the job of creating a soundtrack rather like they did in silent films. Little did I know of the illustrious career the man I was working with enjoyed, as MP, member of the House of Lords and a Knight of the Garter, no less.

Another interesting project I embraced was editing a film of the Calgary Stampede – a sort of Canadian Wild West show – that had been shot by Billy Smart, the famous circus owner, also an impressive character but a very different kettle of fish.

Apart from learning my trade as an editor, I learned another lesson that was to be invaluable in later years. It was the very basic rules of lighting, that you needed a KEY light to illuminate the subject, a FILLER to soften the shadows and a BACK light to separate the subject from the background. But perhaps most important of all was the basic rule of physics that I had learned at school: the angle of incidence equals the angle of reflection.

Filming in the open air is simply a question of getting the exposure right, but in a studio you have to arrange the lights to get the correct result. The first time I was a studio cameraman on my own was to film an interview in our small studio with the then-secretary of the Communist Party, Harry Pollitt. Where the interview would have been shown, I have no idea. There were no political broadcasts at that time, so presumably in working men's clubs or union offices.

I gained a working knowledge of lighting which was to prove superior to several very expensive cameramen I was to employ in years to come. You would be surprised at the number of cameramen, earning fees in excess of £1,000 per day on commercials, who just did not know where to put the lamp to, for example, create a specific highlight on a round object. Worse still was a cameraman who cost me a whole day of filming because he did not know how a reflex camera worked.

If I may be permitted to explain, I have already said that I had learned the basic rules of light at school, and that is why I knew exactly what to do when my cameraman did not. On one occasion, I was producing a commercial for a deodorant spray on location and we were shooting the pack shot in someone's kitchen. The client wanted a simple shot of the can on a plain background (easily arranged with a roll of craft paper), but he also expected a highlight to emphasise the round shape of the can. The cameraman could not produce the right effect, so I took charge and asked the housewife if she had a roll of kitchen foil. By pointing a light at the foil roll and positioning it to reflect in the side of the pack, the desired effect was instantaneous.

I was to make industrial documentaries on two coal marshalling yards for an engineering company, Marshalls, one in Scotland and one at Leicester power station. Then there was a documentary for the CWS canning factory demonstrating the preparation, canning and sterilisation processes at their factory in Lowestoft. It meant I had to film at the top of the sterilising chamber in a temperature in excess of 127 degrees.

It was soon time for my twenty-first birthday, and I arranged a dinner in London at a nightclub and we took Graham, my friend from the army, and Jean, Shirley's oldest and dearest friend.

Our social life revolved around school friends and the sports club in West Wickham to which Shirley had once belonged. There were weekly meetings for coffee at Verneys restaurant in Beckenham High Street and the occasional dance at the Shirley Poppy.

Not all the work at UMP was industrial. I also filmed the procession for the funeral of King George VI, the arrival of Premiers Khruschev and Bulganin at the Guildhall, and covered the Henley Regatta. These events represented a welcome break from the usual industrial subjects. The company was doing well and took a lease on another building in Wardour Street to accommodate more cutting rooms. I had already built new benches for the recording studio and made other alterations to the offices when I was asked to design and make the editing benches complete with light boxes for the new rooms. I got to know the timber yard in Poland Street and hardware store Matthews in Charing Cross Road and elsewhere in Soho. There was also a colour merchant, Hopkins Purvis, in Greek Street, where they mixed your paint for you. It later became a restaurant, but to this day retains the crane arm on the first floor used to raise deliveries to that level. In those days, Soho was very much the village it had been before the war, with very few changes since the 1930s. Traditional trades were still to be found, a tobacconist shop and a watchmaker are two I remember well.

Time was marching on and in 1956 Shirley and I were married in St Georges Church, Beckenham. We were both twenty-two years old. We had been on holiday together the year before when we stayed at the Shanklin Towers Hotel on the Isle of Wight. We had separate rooms, as was the custom in those days!

At UMP we made documentaries for Wolf Electric Tools and Black and Decker in what was a wonderful training for both my eventual career and DIY ambitions. It was to leave me with a lasting memento. Working as a cameraman very close to power saws when cutting sheet or corrugated asbestos resulted in pleural plaque in my lungs. I am very fortunate that it has never become aggressive.

One project I recall in detail started with my being asked to accompany my boss, Jack Shepard, to visit a local builder in Lancing, Sussex. We met in a seafront restaurant and the builder, whose name was Middleton, drove up in a black and red Ford Zephyr with white wall tyres which I thought meant he was probably quite successful, if a little flash! The proposal was to film on a building site where he was using a new product that he had developed that enabled dry wall plastering, saving several weeks of drying out time on new builds. We took the job and I and one other colleague filmed for two days. We wanted a dramatic opening sequence over which to superimpose the titles, so we found a street of smart houses and filmed a tracking shot from the roof of our Dormobile. I had no driving licence at the time, so I climbed onto the roof with the camera while my colleague drove slowly along the street. Back in the studio the film was wound back and the titles successfully superimposed.

Probably *not* as a result of our film, the product became a runaway success. The name of the product? ARTEX.

The advent of commercial television was eagerly awaited and in the run up we were asked to work on several test commercials and programmes. I particularly remember working on *Muffin the Mule* and documentaries with Barbara Woodhouse and her dogs, including a great Dane called Juno who would carry a small companion around in his mouth. There were also test magazine programmes and I remember one with Jill Craigie, a journalist and wife of Michael Foot.

3

THE NEW MEDIUM

The year 1954 saw a virtual buzz of activity in anticipation of the launch of commercial television the following year. The reaction of advertising agencies was mixed. I suspect those with American parent companies or connections had a fair idea of what was coming down the track, and quietly prepared for it. Others were somewhat more sceptical.

The newspaper industry had enjoyed things their own way for quite some time, and many agencies saw this as an opportunity to take them down a peg or two. At the same time there was, I believe, an agency chairman who called a meeting of all his clients to discuss the new medium. Seemingly, it was his contention that "the introduction of messages into the homes of the masses might create an over-awareness of advertising that would – or could – work against the established acceptance of it."

Ironically, the agency later became very successful in TV advertising.

It is not true to say that there was no film advertising in the UK before ITV, as both Rank and Pearl & Dean, who between them controlled the advertising on most of our cinema screens, were screening ads in the cinema chains of the day and they, along with many small documentary companies, probably saw this as the goose that would lay the golden egg.

They had not thought it through!

The film industry had not really changed much since before the war, and was dominated by large studios that had all the facilities in-house: camera department, sound department, lighting and, of course, construction crews. They were bound by ironclad agreements with the unions that operated a closed shop that strictly limited any creative input from the new production companies. To make matters worse, there were three unions to negotiate with and they all had slightly different agreements, even different working hours.

The Association of Cinematograph Technicians (ACT) controlled camera and sound crews, NATKE, the National Association of Theatrical and Kine Employees looked after hairdressers, makeup artistes, wardrobe and props. Finally, there was the ETU, the Electricians Trade Union. To give you an insight into the minefield of ridiculous regulations we had to contend with, the following might be of help. You had to have a meeting with the shop steward before filming started to agree the studio crew that would be allocated to your production. Overtime had to be requested and agreed in advance, at least two hours before it was needed, and if you did not get it and ran over, the electricians were capable of turning off the lights and walking off the set. Not at the end of the working day but ten minutes earlier, as they had a ten-minute washing break negotiated by their union. It was only to happen to me once at ABPC, the studio in Boreham Wood. But once was more than enough. It was time for a change and that change came about almost entirely because of the influence of television commercials.

In the early fifties, a cameraman named Sydney Samuelson – now Sir Sydney – used the money he and his wife had saved for the deposit on a house to buy a clockwork Newman & Sinclair camera. He was more than happy to loan it to other cameramen when he was out of work, and by 1954 he had bought a second camera, and now involved his brothers in the venture. By the end of the century, Samuelson Film Services had become a multinational company supplying film equipment and lighting to a vast variety of film companies, both small and large. I remember in 1954-ish hiring that very camera and collecting it from Sydney's home in Hendon, where, I believe, it was kept in an ex-army wardrobe.

Fortunately for the industry, smaller and much more flexible studios began to spring up, often in abandoned churches. There was one in Carlton Hill Maida Vale, one in St John's Wood and another in the Marylebone Road. Soon they were to be joined by many other small studios, mainly in and around Soho.

Shirley and I started married life in a flat in Tunbridge Wells. We were both working in London and it was only a short walk to the station where the weekly ticket to

London cost twenty-eight shillings. We used to travel in in the morning with other regular commuters and got to know one couple, Jean and Stuart, who had a young child at the time. They were later to emigrate to Australia, and we were to become godparents to their daughter. We were fortunate to be able to visit her and her family several times at their home in Melbourne.

There was one other fellow traveller who was a regular companion on the journey. I am afraid I don't remember his name, but I do recall his most tragic passing. On 4 December, 1957 there was a serious rail crash at Hither Green on our line, which resulted in 97 deaths. Shirley had already reached home as she had taken an earlier train, but she would know that I would be on the one that crashed. As the evening was very foggy, I knew that my regular train from Charing Cross would be late, so I made a quick decision to take the tube to Cannon Street, and try and catch an earlier service. I made it in time, but the crash meant that all traffic was halted and the power cut off. There was no way of letting Shirley know that I was safe. So she faced a long and anxious wait, comforted by the elderly neighbours in the flat across the landing from ours.

My daily travelling companion was killed and I could well have been with him.

In late 1957, my father-in-law asked us if we would be interested in a rental property in Chelsfield. Shirley's father worked for Child & Co., the UK's oldest bank. He was based in Fleet Street and lunched most days with someone who was the company secretary of a development company.

The company concerned was called Homesteads, and they had developed a large area close to the village of Chelsfield during the 1930s. Most of the houses had been sold, but there was one left, with a tenant. The tenant was an accountant who had lived there since it was built and now wanted to buy it. He had taken no interest in the property in all the years there, so the company refused to sell to him. And that's how it came to be offered to us.

We saw the property on a grey November day, and it was pretty depressing. I would describe the paint as "public lavatory green". There were still gaslights on the landing, and a pretty disgusting gas geyser over the bath. I have always had the ability to see beyond the surface and soon realised the enormous potential of the place. We immediately accepted and moved in with a three-year rental agreement at two pounds ten shillings a week. The house stood on a three-quarter acre plot, and had three bedrooms and a garage. At the bottom of the garden we had access to a tennis club, exclusive to the development.

Every spare minute and extra penny we could summon up was put into that house over the next five or six years. As a result, DIY became part and parcel of our everyday life. I installed a modern electrical system involving the new PVC cables that had just come into use. Previously single cables had to be threaded into small iron pipes. I hand-built a complete new kitchen and made numerous alterations including getting rid of the gas in the bathroom and landing, laying cork floors in the bedrooms, landscaping the garden, and planting many new trees.

On my way to work, I would often walk along Great Marlborough Street and past a showroom of the company, Radiation. They had a display of modern boilers in the window and as I needed to replace the very old boiler in our kitchen, I purchased one with a yellow casing and heavy grey top. It was to be my first venture into plumbing. I visited the local tool shop and bought a couple of pipe wrenches and then made my way to the builders merchant at the top of Orpington high street and purchased the iron pipe fittings, hemp and sealing compound that were needed. The only information I needed to supply was the size of the three sections and distance from the new boiler.

It went perfectly and I never needed to employ the services of a professional plumber until old age and new regulations made it mandatory. Once when I built a new kitchen, I worked to very tight margins and when the gas board installed our new cooker, I found that it fouled the drawer set at right angles on the right-hand side. To my mind, the solution was simple. I took the cooker out and cut the union joint in half, enabling me to put the cooker back just enough to be able to open the drawer. Another major achievement involved the new electricity supply. It had to be inspected by the supply company, and when the inspector arrived the first thing he asked was, "Who was your contractor?" He was not very pleased to be told that I had done it myself, and he proceeded to go through everything with a fine-tooth comb.

Eventually he finished and said to me, "Well, Mr. Forster, I must congratulate you. I have not seen as good a job done by a professional."

From that day on I never employed an electrician.

Why do I bore you with all these details? Because they just happen to illustrate two key elements of my makeup. I am a perfectionist – which may have made me hard to live with on occasion. And I will happily embrace most challenges that come my way. Both elements were to prove very influential in my coming business life.

By 1955, when commercial television was launched, I had already worked on several test commercials and a number of pilot programmes. United Motion Pictures was very well placed to provide editing and dubbing services to the many producers hoping to get screen time on the new medium.

It is important at this point to say that my training in a small documentary production company taught me the basic skills of each and every department of the industry. I was not a union member, and I wouldn't be for many years as they operated a closed shop. So it was only by working in a small company, under the union radar, that I could have gained this wealth of experience.

In 1956, Shirley had a job in a small advertising agency that closed down and she went to work for the Outdoor

Publicity department of a larger firm, the London Press Exchange in St Martin's Lane. Occasionally, Shirley would bring home a copy of the advertising magazine, *Advertisers' Weekly,* and I decided that the new business of television commercials was the challenge I was looking for.

4

COMMERCIAL BREAKS

In an attempt to get a foot in the door of the new medium, I wrote four letters and received two replies, one from an agency offering to keep my letter on file, the other from Pearl & Dean, the cinema advertising giant, granting me an interview.

The eventual interview was with a man called Byron Lloyd, who was, at the time, the Managing Director of Pearl & Dean Production. I was offered a position as a trainee writer/director at a salary of £13 a week. I made the break and joined the company on 13 June, 1957. (Since then, I have always regarded 13 as *my* lucky number.)

It is important to realise that at Pearl & Dean, the production of commercials for their cinema advertising clients was seen as very much a secondary service to the main business of distribution and selling advertising time in cinemas. I, on the other hand, looked upon it as a business in its own right.

As I have said, both Pearl & Dean and Rank, with their experience of cinema advertising, probably saw TV commercials as the goose that would lay the golden egg. Well used to selling direct to local clients and major companies, Pearl & Dean took a lease on a studio and hired a full-time camera, sound crew, set up two model animation units and a cartoon unit, and sent their salesmen out to their established cinema clients and their advertising agencies. Very soon they discovered their mistake. They were dealing with a new medium and no longer controlled the screen.

Pearl & Dean's greatest mistake was to start selling direct to some of their previous cinema clients. By selling direct to a client like Beecham, for instance, they alienated not only the agency handling that particular product, but also the four other agencies handling the other Beecham brands.

I started work sharing an office with two other trainees. We were pretty relaxed and enjoyed a lot of laughter and copious cups of coffee at the Grafton Street coffee bar just around the corner from our office in Berkeley Street. It appeared to be staffed by Debs, just as Anthony Newley had suggested in his song, "Things ain't what they used to be". We were just beginning to see the start of a new era.

I can remember my first-ever script to be accepted by a client. The project was a cinema advertising film for Lux toilet soap. My script was based on a girl looking at her reflection in an ornamental pool, and as rose petals floated down, the voice-over spoke the immortal words, "For that petal-soft fragrance of a lasting beauty." I still cringe at the memory to this today.

The company did not have a suitable director and so they brought in a freelance, Kenneth Hume, a director with a couple of short films to his name. Studio space was unavailable in London, so Ken and our production manager, an Irishman named, Pat Kelly, were sent over to Paris, where a stage was available. Sadly, I was not included! Had I been, the result would have been rather different. Back then, the writer and art director had no say once the script went into production. I was told that the scenes as written could not be photographed, so compromises would need to be made. I knew exactly how to shoot them!

At this time, budgets were prepared by a production manager, not the producer, and were frequently exceeded leaving the producer to explain to the agency or client why more money was needed over and above the quoted price. Looking back, it was perhaps understandable as there were no experienced producers, we were all learning a new trade, but I resolved there and then that if I ever had to quote a price myself, I would stick to it, unless the client demanded last minute changes. This was a decision that would pay enormous dividends in terms of my reputation and standing in the industry in the years to come.

After only a few weeks, the production supervisor, John Hine, who was responsible for producing all the company's commercials, went on holiday and I was asked to stand in for him. For the first time I found myself sitting opposite a secretary with pencil poised as I started in the role of producer. Ken Hume was still working for the company as a freelance, and I found myself producing various commercials with him as my director.

The *Daily Sketch,* with actor Bill Shine, is one I remember (I still have a copy of it on DVD). Bill was an accomplished character actor whose father, mother, grandmother, two uncles and an aunt, were all on the stage. An American named, Monte Landis, was another character actor we made a couple of newspaper commercials with. He would present the paper to camera with the line, "Hold it up to the light, not a bit of news inside it," was a parody of a Daz commercial of the time.

Even in the early years of television commercials, personalities were in demand, and I worked with one or two who were to become very famous in later life. Nicholas Parsons, who went on to become a household name as a game show host and television personality, did a number of commercials for Blue Cars, a coach company. Suzy, his daughter, worked with me for many years as a temporary secretary.

In 1956, a young African-American singer made a breakthrough with his album, *Calypso.* His name was Harry Belafonte and the commercial I produced with him was for the holiday destination of Jersey. Harry was an associate of Martin Luther King and became a UNICEF ambassador. Jess Conrad was a pop singer in the fifties when I worked with him. He later became an actor and was awarded the OBE for services to charity. He was also a member of the Water Rats and became Chief Rat. Somewhat less well known was Regimental Sergeant Major Britain, often referred to as the voice of the British Army, who made a commercial for Black and Decker electric drills. This project marked the first time I used a zoom lens – despite being told it wasn't possible.

Tidysan™, a disposable flooring for bird cages, is another spot I remember well. I also produced one of the very first commercials for Flash, at the time just a floor cleaner. I would go on to produce umpteen commercials for Flash in the future.

I soon had a location shoot away from London. It was a 60-second colour cinema commercial for Capri scooters that involved a group of young people riding around various locations including some of the more expensive residential areas of Brighton and ending up on the sea front. The final scene, as they arrived on the front, featured a full-sized hoarding advertising the scooter, set up on the beach. Did I have permission? Not at all! So it was not too long before a representative from the council turned up and wanted to know what we were doing.

Things were a lot simpler in those days, and it was incredible what a £5 note could achieve. So we carried on regardless and shot the scene as scripted. The young actor who played the lead would one day become a very successful businessman setting up the Lighting Emporium in the King's Road. It is strange to find that Brighton has become the venue for an annual reunion of scooter owners.

Another time, I was producing a commercial for Arrow shirts and was scheduled for a three-day set build. We were scheduled to film on the Monday, but, of course, the set build overran and a check on the final time sheets revealed – to my horror – that there had been a crew of three during the week, as well as twelve or thirteen on Saturday and Sunday at double time! The effect on the budget was disastrous, and I had been well and truly stitched up. The Studio, St John's Wood, or rather the man who owned it, gained a reputation that ultimately proved to be his downfall.

It was not to be too many years before demand from the agencies led to better directors leaving the larger companies and setting up on their own. In the late fifties and sixties, there were many companies going bust. The problem was it was all well and good to let a talented director set up a company – which was becoming easy with the growth of freelance suppliers – but without a strong producer to look after the business end and the viability of the contracts, they were very often destined to fail.

More of that later.

Most advertising agencies embraced the new television medium with enthusiasm and one in particular put under contract some very senior members of the film industry in an attempt to corner the market. At first the relationship between commercials and feature films was somewhat strained as the former was seen as very much the poor relation. Many senior technicians felt it was prostituting their art to admit to working on advertising.

There was no separate union agreement for commercials, so if you were shooting sound, you were committed to a crew of twelve union members, at least two of whom had nothing to do. Gradually commercials became an accepted source of work (and income) for feature directors and cameramen, many of whom made a very real contribution to the industry. It was not always quite as simple as it might have been. The demands of commercials in terms of timing and the framing of scenes were totally different to those of feature films. It was customary in the early days for a cameraman to always work with his regular crew, but this soon became a problem. After shooting a car commercial in a studio, I immediately noticed the reflection of the camera on the side of the car in the rushes. What's more, two petrol pumps that were supposed to end up being symmetrical, with one on either side of the final shot, were off line, so I had to tell an Academy Award-winning cameraman that I could not employ his operator again.

Today we accept that modern electronic wizardry can change literally any element of a filmed image. This was not always the case and television was still fairly basic and could not produce a clean black and white image. The range had to be compressed into an image that the early transmitters and sets could cope with. I had already learned this at the lecture I attended on densitometry in my early days at UMP.

So how did the early broadcasters cope with the problem? Newscasters in those days would be seen wearing evening dress, but their dinner jackets were blue and their white shirts blue or yellow. A year or two later, I was to make a Persil commercial with the line "Persil washes whiter and it shows" – the white shirt was shown in shades of grey.

Studio lights were a problem as they generated a great deal of heat making it impossible to photograph something like ice. The very first commercial – for Gibbs SR toothpaste – actually featured a block of ice.

The ice melted under the lights and also clouded so that you could not see the product. I believe that commercial cost the advertiser £24,000, which was given to charity. In the first year of TV advertising, the revenue amounted to £2.4 million. By 2010 that figure had jumped to £1.45 billion. By this time the senior company rep, and a director of the company, Tony Solomon, was singling me out to produce any work he brought in. This was to the detriment of the production supervisor whose work I was taking over. What happened to the fellow whose job I took over on a temporary basis? He found a job in an agency. Small wonder I was never to get work from him as an agency producer.

One of the very first commercials I produced was for Bristows lanolin shampoo for Immedia, the television department of the agency LPE. This resulted in an invitation to join the agency as a senior producer. I had an interview with their head of television, Pat Lynott, but unfortunately it was the company that Shirley was working for in their Outdoor Advertising department and company policy did not allow the employment of husbands and wives. Perhaps this was fortuitous, but I will never know!

I was now very busy and enjoying my new occupation, but at home the work had really started.

Pearl & Dean had a very successful cartoon unit housed in a separate building at 38 Dover Street. It had a good reputation and plenty of work and was certainly the largest animation unit in the commercial field at the time. It had a staff of sixty. There were two key animators, George Moreno, who had worked for Disney in the U.S., and Fred Thompson, an English animator, along with teams of trace and paint artists, a rostrum camera department, and a full cutting room staff.

One day I was asked by the chairman to act as holiday relief for the man in charge of the unit, an ex-naval officer named Harry Poustie. This was to give me my first experience of serious cartoon production. The unit was responsible for some very high profile campaigns in the early days, including the Oxo man, Murray Mints, Rael Brook Shirts, and many more. When I took over the office, there were three very important productions due for delivery within the next two weeks, but there was a problem. (Isn't there always?) A strike was looming and I very quickly had to get to know not only the staff but the problem and, most importantly, the shop steward, our negative cutter, Nancy Treadwell.

I used all my powers of persuasion and charm and somehow averted the strike. I cannot remember what the problem was but, in retrospect, I suspect that I had been landed in that situation thanks to Ernie Pearl, and the head of the unit may well have been sent on holiday. Being an ex-naval officer, he was possibly not the best person to deal with a strike. Be that as it may, the strike was averted and the delivery dates met.

Years later I was to face another potential strike, but I will come to that in due course.

Shirley and I had moved into the house in Chelsfield. It needed a lot of work but I was already becoming a dab hand at DIY. Around the same time, a project came my way that ultimately proved very useful. The company was asked to produce a commercial for Crown wallpapers, and one day I was called into Byron's office and told to take a young man from the agency in Manchester out to lunch. I was given cash and told that a table had been booked at a restaurant in Dover Street. It was the start of my business entertaining which was to go on uninterrupted for the next forty-five years. The young man in question was none other than Peter Marsh, who later became a client of mine when he ran his own agency, Allen Brady and Marsh. (Not many people know that he married young, the first time to an actress who played Elsie Tanner in *Coronation Street*, Pat Phoenix.) The shoot completed, I was left with dozens of rolls of different wallpapers, and so the conversion of our 1930s house into a contemporary showpiece began.

P&D decided to offer Ken Hume a contract and, much to my surprise, he agreed on condition that I would be his producer. Ken was not untalented, but up to that time his only claim to fame had been a couple of very minor productions, one called *Elephant Boy*, shot in India, and another shot in the UK called *Green Ice*. As far as I know both sank without trace.

After accepting the contract offered by the company, Ken and I were given a suite of offices on the second floor of the company block at 17 Berkeley Street.

P&D had two blocks of old mansion flats back-to-back between Berkeley Street and Dover Street. They also had other offices in another building in Dover Street (the animation unit) and in Half Moon Street.

Ken brought in a designer friend and the suite was transformed into an ultra-contemporary office with a wide black and white striped floor, hessian covered walls and a false ceiling. The main door was upholstered in imitation leather with the initials KH in six-inch high brass letters, something I copied from the brass UMP I had made and mounted at that company.

We were known as the Kenneth Hume Unit, and were increasingly successful.

We established a good relationship with the Foote Cone and Belding agency, and made many commercials for them. We made two spots for Fry's Chocolate Medley bars with a jingle sung and danced to by Dougie Squires. One we filmed on the old West Pier in Brighton, the other in a new office block in St Martin's Lane. For a time all went well until Ken reasoned that we could do a lot better by working for ourselves. He borrowed £7,000 from an American by the name of Bobby Kidde, who worked at the Embassy in Grosvenor Square. He then immediately bought a gold Bentley Continental convertible and used various contacts to find and equip an office at 169 Wardour Street in Soho for the new company, Kenneth Hume Productions.

In 1959, Shirley and I had a lot on our plates. Work on the new house was practically a full-time job. We also found ourselves pregnant, to boot. Hardly the ideal time to give up a steady job.

5

SETTING RECORDS

Also in 1959, we very sadly lost our first child, but our daughter, Sarah, was born the following year.

The company was very successful and we had an excellent staff that included an editor from Pearl & Dean and, at one time, the brother of Adam Faith, Roger Nelhams, who was sadly killed some time later in a motorcycle accident. We built a very strong relationship with several agencies, particularly Armstrong Warden, where the creative director, Ron Garbett, became a great friend. I think it was the very first job for that agency that was to cause me a real problem.

The agency had written a commercial for Schick razors with a sung jingle that ended with the phrase, "Start the day right with a Schick", which we pointed out could be the subject of unwanted comments. The agency had wanted a well-known singer and had a budget of ten thousand pounds. Ken said that he knew the singer and could get him for that sum.

He actually paid only five thousand and kept the rest. I visited the singer at his house in the Bishops Avenue in Addington to deliver the script and cash on my way home.

Not many months later the man was dead, he had committed suicide. I am not suggesting the incident had any bearing on his death, but it left a bad taste and became something I would never forget

At the time, the film industry was ruled by the unions (the A.C.T., N.A.T.K.E. and the ETU) and you had to employ union members in every category. I very soon became aware that a hairdresser who might have been excellent at reproducing period styles for a feature film was more often than not totally wrong for the demands of the commercial client. I set about finding union members who had previous salon experience and this helped us establish a growing number of clients in that particular area.

Other agencies we had strong relationships with included Legget Nicholson and Partners where the producer was Claude Lipscombe, and Foote Cone and Belding, where we were to work for all of the four producers on such brands as Gibbs shampoo, Electrolux and Fry's chocolate products.

Perhaps our most memorable commercials were for BOAC, who wanted to promote two aircraft in their fleet, the Comet and the new Boeing 707. The idea was to create an aerial ballet, making two 60-second commercials, one for each plane. Putting a plane in the air is an expensive business, but BOAC was prepared to allocate each plane to us for three hours. The next problem we faced was not where to film them but how. We could fly out over the sea but we needed another plane as a camera platform. So we eventually decided to use a Bristol Britannia and take out some of the windows so that our three cameras would not be looking through plastic. That meant that the plane could not be pressurised so our height was restricted to 10,000 feet, adding more cost to the operation of the subject jets.

We achieved some really dramatic footage but the best plane from our point of view was the Comet, which was a very graceful aircraft. We were able to fill the screen with the silver underbelly before the plane would peel off into the distance. That particular shot never worked quite as well with the Boeing. When the material was edited and set to a Ray Conniff music track, the result was dramatic. Some time after the shoot, I discovered that BOAC had given staff the opportunity to fly in both planes, but those in the Boeing had a rough ride as it just was not as maneuverable as the Comet.

Other memorable jobs included Harp Lager and Fry's Walnut Whip. On both shoots we used a brilliant art director, Alan Withey, who could do amazing things in a small space with false perspective. Or was it forced? One of our earliest commercials was for the English furniture manufacturer, Greaves and Thomas. The idea was simple, show English furniture in an English parkland setting and we chose Woburn Abbey, the home of the Duke of Bedford. Many years later, I was to work with the Duke when he agreed to make a commercial for American Express. Filming went very well until our generator, that weighed perhaps ten tons, drove across a grass area that suddenly gave way. Apparently a tree had been felled there a few weeks earlier and the ground had not been compacted.

The next year, Ken was approached by an old friend, a former production manager who ran a book and art shop in West Hampstead with his wife. They said they needed a loan of £6,000. We had a meeting and soon realised that what was needed was a great deal more and Ken agreed to take over the company. Straight away I discovered that the company had kept no books and had taken over the liabilities of a previous partnership.

I found that the wife, who worked in the shop, was paying herself from the till and the extent of the debts was not being disclosed to me. I had to take immediate action and put the lady on emergency tax and had all the mail redirected to our office in Wardour Street. Between commercials, I contacted every supplier and established the amount of the debts and when they were incurred. I eventually produced a set of accounts that were accepted by the Inland Revenue as the basis for the company. Unfortunately, the shop was in West End Lane, West Hampstead, which was not a good area, situated as it was between Finchley Road and Maida Vale.

The only plus for me was that I became very friendly with the bank manager next door. Once when he asked if I wanted another overdraft, he just gave me a chequebook and said to let him know what I filled it in for. He must have had faith in me. The relationship lasted for some thirty years, but those were the days of real bank managers.

A better way of bringing business into the shop was clearly needed. The answer was to arrive in a very dramatic and surprising way. Life with Ken as a partner had its ups and downs. He could be very generous and very amusing, but it was not all fun and games and he could, and frequently did, go off on a tangent at times.

There were times when I would receive a call at home on a Saturday morning to go into London and clear a cheque at our bank, Barclays in The Strand. There were other occasions when I had two men in raincoats looking all the world like associates of the Kray twins (which they could very well have been) waiting for hours in the office to see if Ken would turn up.

He never did.

So how was I going to turn around the fortunes of the shop? I was in the office one morning when I took a call from the *Daily Mirror* asking me to confirm that Ken had got married. I genuinely did not know anything about it and denied it. Later I discovered that it was true and that he had married Shirley Bassey. Ken had married Shirley B. on 8 June, 1961, and almost immediately we were due to fly to Cannes for the annual advertising film festival. So, in effect, Shirley (my Shirley, that is) and I with one small daughter were going with the newly married couple on their honeymoon.

I was landed with more work as Ken had bought a house in Carlton Hill, Maida Vale and wanted some alterations made including new units in the kitchen/dining room. I was soon on the case but, with no DIY supermarkets in those days, it was not easy to find the units I wanted. I eventually managed to get them from a builders merchant in Penge in South East London.

At about this time we were commissioned to make a commercial for a rice dessert product and needed to work with a special effects team in Shepperton Studios. I drove to Shepperton in the company car, a light grey Mini 195 BLH. As I approached a right turn into the Studios – clearly indicating my intention – I was struck by a car coming out of the turning that then drove off. I noted his number plate and another driver offered himself as a witness. I reported the incident en route home to the station sergeant at Penge police station. To my surprise, the sergeant said he knew who owned the car and told me the registered owner. Armed with this information, I expected everything to be straightforward. It was to be anything but.

Eventually we got a letter from Scotland Yard informing us that the driver of the car had not been traced. Bearing in mind we knew who owned the vehicle, we told the police that we would take the matter to the Sunday papers and were accused of threatening the police. Meanwhile, I took matters up with the AA and was told to drop my claim. To cut a long story short, eventually the driver was found, and two days before the court case, he pleaded guilty.

We employed a second secretary to look after Shirley B., and quickly found that she had no official fan club but that mail was coming into her record company, EMI. It made me think that we might possibly be able to convert the room at the rear of the shop into a record shop.

At this time, there was a studio and prop hire company owned by a man called Roy Moore based in Isleworth, and he discussed with us a scheme for purchasing a large amount of surplus stock from a well-known furniture retailer, Harrison Gibson, and using it to furnish flats and set up a property rental business. Thank goodness that scheme never came to fruition and I became very suspicious when one of the two stores was burned down a year or two later. Ironically, I had produced a commercial for the company and met the chief executive when, in the absence of the agency producer, I found myself in the agency to present the work. He suggested a change and I agreed with him. This rather confused the agency as they had assumed I would defend the cut at all costs. Quite simply, the alteration he asked for was sensible and correct. I was, after all, in the advertising business, not the film industry.

In the meantime we were starting production on a pilot for a television series about a lady detective. It was to be called *The Secret Keepers*, and had a great song as its signature tune. The star role was to be played by Alma Cogan and I remember my first meeting with her in her flat on Kensington High Street, where there were several famous character actors including Cardew Robinson and Frankie Howerd, to name but two. Ken had promised Shirley B. an entry to a film career but this was hardly it, she was to play a street singer.

One lasting personal memory is of Frankie Howerd suggesting that I accompany him to Paris for the weekend! What he had in mind I do not know.

About this time, we were commissioned to make a commercial for Supersoft shampoo. The script was loosely based on Excalibur, and we had two knights in armour mounted on fully-dressed horses. The location was the lake at Virginia Water and one of the knights had to fall into the shallow lake. The armour didn't present a problem as it was plastic and very light, not so the chain mail underneath it. It was not, of course, real chain but rather knitted string and as soon as it got wet it started to shrink causing a frantic search for scissors to release our actor.

Another client we worked for was one of the large bakery chains. The commercial had the line "Bakers eat it", and the script featured a countryside scene with several young riders in a stable yard setting. At one point, one of the young riders was thrown from her horse and had to receive medical attention. We were using a couple of arc lights and later I wondered whether the striking (lighting) of one of the lights might have spooked her horse.

But let's get back to our solution for the ailing shop. After much thought, I set about converting the rear of the shop into a record shop. I was working in the evenings but had to stop at about 11 pm as there were flats upstairs. One night on the drive home, I was woken by a fellow driver frantically beeping his horn as he passed me – on the passenger side. I was driving at 50 mph on the wrong side of the road at 2 am!

The space was quite large and we built two soundproof booths and a glass-topped counter with three turntables, and all the necessary shelving. Stocking the new shop was not a problem as we had established a very good relationship with EMI and other suppliers. To staff it we employed a young woman who had worked for NEMS in Liverpool, and an older lady (Dorothy States) recently widowed, who was introduced to us by our bank manager.

In a relatively short time, the shop opened as Shirley's Record Shop. It was to have limited success due to its position and that meant further thought was needed. I never questioned where money was coming from, but it must have been from Shirley B. Despite the fact that we were still making commercials, I do not remember any major commitments and when we had to pay money to Ken to cover the latest gambling losses, I simply put them down to his personal account.

I soon came to realise that the letters Shirley B. was receiving gave us an opportunity to sell her records direct to her fans, and that made me believe that if we could contact other stars' fan bases, we might be able to create a rather substantial mail order business. The problem was how to contact the fans without it costing money. I knew we could count on the record companies, but when I discovered official fan clubs sent out regular newsletters, things really fell into place.

The retail record business was subject to a scheme known as Retail Price Maintenance, which meant that you could not discount their products. So what incentive could we offer fan clubs to sign up with us? The answer was simple. We could give the clubs a commission on any sales they generated. The shop had an unused basement that provided the area needed to operate the scheme and very quickly I outlined how it could work. We had the cooperation of the record companies who would deliver records to us for posting the day before the official release, so the records would arrive with the fans on the release date. It was simple, the clubs would deliver our order forms with their newsletters and when they were returned to us they would be numbered and tallies kept for each club to calculate commission payments. Any order for an LP would automatically get a photo of the star and there would be a monthly prize draw. Simple cardboard sleeves meant that packing and postage was no problem, and, of course, we would be getting cash in advance. It seemed the perfect solution to the problem of bringing in more cash and making full use of the available space. I started contacting various managements and had my first meeting with the manager of a well-known singer in a basement flat just off Portland Square. That deal done I moved on and the second club that I signed up was the Frank Sinatra Appreciation Society.

Ken got involved with someone who was running a scheme called the Commonwealth Readers Service, which employed students to sell magazine subscriptions door-to-door and earn points to go towards funds to help offset their university fees. How much cash ever reached them I do not know. There was a question in Parliament about the scheme, but I do not recall the result. What people did not know when they signed up to receive monthly copies of an expensive glossy magazine was the publishers were only interested in one thing, the circulation figures that would allow them to increase their advertising rates.

My partnership with Ken had always been based on him being the creative one, while I swept up the debris and kept the partnership on an even keel. The scheme that Ken now came up with involved putting together a package of religious books and records and selling them to unsuspecting housewives door-to-door. Jumping the gun slightly, Ken employed a young man as a salesman and I had to provide him with a car and a petrol account. There were three books to cover the three main denominations: Anglican, Catholic, and Jewish.

The Anglican books came from one of the newspaper companies that had massively over printed them and just wanted to offload them. They were respectable enough with white imitation leather bindings and I think we were getting them for about ten shillings each. Gospel records from America were added to the package. Again very cheap to buy and the whole package was to be sold at something like £20. The deal was to be financed by English and Overseas Finance, a company owned by John Bloom, who had made his name with cheap washing machines. I held my first meeting with him in the London Clinic where he was undergoing treatment.

After my meeting with John Bloom, I was becoming increasingly concerned with the whole business. I had to dismiss the salesman Ken had employed as he was just costing us money and had no real job, so I had to get the car and the petrol account card back.

A meeting was arranged for 3 pm one day at our solicitor, David Jacobs, to finalise the structure and formalise the new company. I was not prepared to go ahead, but had no clear idea of what I was going to do. I had not forgotten Schick razors.

6

PRINCIPLES MATTER

What it came down to was a simple matter of principle. You could bend your principles now and then, but in the end you had to stand up and be counted. And I had reached that point.

I was of course still producing commercials when all this was going on. As I walked along Piccadilly at 9 am the day before our scheduled meeting on my way to an advertising agency, a car pulled up in front of me, the driver sounding its horn. It was Jack Dean, the younger brother of Bob Dean, joint founder of Pearl & Dean, offering me a lift. I accepted and he immediately asked, "When are you going to come back?" "You could not afford me," I replied. He persisted, "How much do you want?" "Two thousand a year!" I blurted out.

We arranged to meet for lunch at Brown's Hotel in Dover Street the next day and, following a P&D board meeting that morning, I accepted an offer from P&D on the very day of the meeting to set the other venture in motion. To this day I can hardly believe the timing of our meeting. It was really quite extraordinary. But the offer and a good lunch meant that I went straight from the restaurant to the meeting and immediately resigned from all companies.

A few days later, I rejoined Pearl & Dean at the Cannes Advertising Film Festival. The day I returned was our seventh wedding anniversary. How do I know that? I arrived home with a large bunch of flowers that were not an anniversary present. I had forgotten our anniversary. That marked the last time I ever did!

A year or two after I parted company with Ken, I was shocked to hear he had committed suicide. Whether it was intentional or an accidental overdose, I don't know. I was abroad at the time.

The date was 25 June, 1967.

I returned to Pearl & Dean as producer with the intention of improving the image of the company and building up the television production side of the business. To cut a long story short, I was successful and virtually tripled the turnover of the P&D production company. The real problem was, as I have already said, that production was seen as merely an aid to selling time on cinema screens, whereas I saw it as a profit centre in its own right. Long gone were the days when directors were employees, they were now mostly freelance. During my first spell at P&D, I had had to produce three commercials on one day, which meant that clients were liable to be kept waiting for their turn.

On one particular day, the first commercial was for Weatherlux Dhobi raincoats and featured four masked men wearing the product in a dance routine with umbrellas.

Next, after lunch was a colour cinema commercial for Morris cars with a young couple and the line "Together, we chose a Morris". Last, but not least, was a commercial for Focus hair colouring featuring a young model, Sandra Paul. Sandra, as I write this, is the wife of the one-time leader of the Conservative Party, Michael Howard. Not surprisingly perhaps, the Focus commercial was not well prepared and had to be reshot.

Those days were gone, never to return. The industry had grown up but I was in a company with no track record in commercial production. This made it difficult to attract the talent that would be needed if I were to change the image of the company. I needed to find a director, but knew it was not going to be easy. Eventually I found someone, but always knew that it would only be the first step on a long road.

Several new companies had started up but I was up against two in particular, Rank Screen Services and Anglo Scottish. There were three executives all seeking to improve their company images and I was the youngest. While my competitors advertised frequently in the trade magazines, I spent my first six months getting to know my staff and making sure they were, as far as was possible, round pegs in round holes. I also reviewed the salaries and got a few anomalies put right. If I was to succeed, the staff had to be kept happy and work well together. Of the three executives charged with revitalising their companies, I was by far the most successful, substantially increasing turnover and gradually improving our image.

Cigarettes and tobacco were among the biggest advertisers at that time and, over the course of the next year or two, I worked on some ten or more brands. I even became a smoker myself! One of the first commercials to be directed by my new director was for a mentholated cigarette, and was commissioned by BAT, the British American Tobacco company direct.

The first issue we faced was casting. It was always a problem to find young good-looking people of either gender willing to appear in cigarette adverts. On this occasion, I held many casting sessions with a representative of the client, seeing everyone in my rather large office in Berkeley Street. One young man appeared with a classic comb-over hairstyle, and when he left, I made a remark to the effect that I could never employ anyone like that. Then I happened to glance at my client's hair, or rather lack of it, and wanted to fall through the floor. Oops!

The script called for spectacular scenery and water, and as my director was in contact with a very good French cameraman, he was employed. We decided on a French chateau with fountains – a most apt metaphor for a mentholated cigarette – as our location. The director, cameraman and client set off for France to find a location. The rest of the crew would join them once the location had been agreed. Was it my unfortunate remark to the client or just bad luck? They spent longer than should have been necessary to agree a chateau, and then said they had to re-plumb the fountain and sent for more money. Eventually filming was finished and the unit returned. When the rushes were seen, the client said it looked as though it had been shot on the banks of the Grand Union Canal.

More footage was shot in Kensington Gardens, but I took the bull by the horns and refunded a substantial sum of money to the company, a step that did me no harm. I cannot recall any of the other commercials that director was responsible for, and he was not around for very much longer.

Apart from directors, I needed to find at least one new producer. The obvious source in those days was the feature film industry and it provided me with about three new employees. True, they would probably leave if a new offer of work on a feature came up, but at least they were experienced. One of the first I employed was Tom Pevsner, who had just returned from a spell as an assistant director on a film in Jamaica and was looking for his next job. He was the son of Nikolaus Pevsner, the well-known architectural historian. Another appointment was an Irish-born assistant director I shall call Mick, having forgotten his name, but not his exploits.

One of the historical clients of Pearl & Dean was Ovaltine, and we were charged with producing at least two cinema commercials each year. As luck would have it, it became my responsibility to come up with the ideas. We made commercials with the Cornish fishermen in Mevagissey, with the construction crew building the new Victoria underground line, and even sponsored Captain Blashford-Snell of the Royal Military Academy

Sandhurst on an expedition up the Nile. We featured a BBC disc jockey and once made a commercial with Radio Caroline, the pirate radio station in the North Sea. I think that Ovaltine was probably a sponsor of the Olympics and in 1964 the Winter Games were taking place in Innsbruck, Austria. I sent Mick, the Irish producer, off with a camera unit to get what coverage he could without any official clearance or permission.

Some scenes were covered from a ski lift and other more general footage was not too much of a problem. Then he pulled a masterstroke. Getting up well before dawn, he took up a position on an official press stand before anyone else arrived. Good coverage was achieved before he was arrested, but the focus puller managed to walk away with the completed footage.

As I have already said, actual production was seen as a service to selling space on cinema screens and that had to change. The other companies in the group, whether international or local, had to pay the full price of the services they were receiving. I was not always popular, and as I was entitled to have lunch in the directors' dining room, there were occasions when nobody would talk to me. More than once, when I crossed swords with one of the directors over some perceived error, I would say, "I am happy to tell the chairman." And I always did, thereby taking the wind out of the sails of my opponent.

In 1965, Pearl & Dean was experiencing problems with its company in Greece, and I was asked by the chairman to go out there, investigate and report back.

The problem was the relationship between an English director, Hugh Ramsey, and his Greek Managing Director, Neo Sophroniou. On arrival in Athens, I was greeted by the MD and treated like visiting royalty from head office. Each day I was bombarded with criticism by one or other of the parties, and I began to feel a bit like a pendulum swinging first towards the MD, then back towards the director.

Eventually, of course, I could see through the arguments and after visiting all the advertising agencies the company had worked with, I had a pretty good idea of what my recommendations would be. For the duration of my stay, I was in a small hotel on the main square in front of the Old Royal Palace. I was suffering from a nervous stomach made worse by the tension of my situation, and I took a medicine now I suspect banned, Dr. Collis Browne's Chlorodine. Heaven only knows what it contained.

On the penultimate day of my visit, in a thinly-veiled attempt to influence my report, I was asked by Neo if I would like to accompany him on a visit to a local office in Rhodes. We flew out and checked into a modern hotel during a rainstorm. The roof was leaking and in reception numerous buckets were deployed on the floor to catch the drips. We set out on the short journey to the local office that seemed to be housed in the local fish market. What a smell! I was introduced to the local manager who thought I was much more important than I was feeling. I was also introduced to his secretary before being taken on a tour of the local cinema in the middle of a performance. We were to have dinner that evening with the manager and the secretary was invited to join us, but only after we had visited her parents to get their permission. We dined in what looked like a small Martello tower, with a small concrete dance floor and a four-piece band playing the latest Beatles' hits rather badly. I spent a very uncomfortable evening refusing to get up and dance with the only girl in the party. Next morning we were at the airport to catch the first flight back to Athens when I got a telephone call. It was the secretary wanting to say goodbye and asking me to send her postcards from London.

Back in London, one of the employees, Jim Pettet, looked after productions that were being made for overseas clients and handled work for the Geneva office of Procter & Gamble. I cannot remember just how it came about but I very soon took over his client and developed a very strong relationship with the company that was to last for some thirty-five years. The Geneva office handled mainly projects for the Middle East and African markets, and very soon I was making frequent trips to 80 Rue de Lausanne, Geneva to be briefed on new projects. Eventually I would write many of the scripts myself.

The advertising department was headed by a pleasant American, Bill Bowld. His assistant and my client was a small bundle of energy called Nicky, or to be more accurate, Niklaus E. Otto. Nicky was Hungarian by birth, but had left his homeland during the uprising in 1956. He and I enjoyed one another's company immensely, both in London where we would often drop into the bar at the Mayfair Hotel for a whisky mac after meetings, and on my many trips to Geneva.

There was an amusing incident one evening when two women were talking in Hungarian at the bar. After some minutes, they got the shock of their lives when this businessman joined in the conversation in their own language.

I was entrusted with a number of secret projects for P&G and through writing, producing and then presenting them, I came to know many of the senior management. I also became something of an expert in producing Arabic commercials in England and had contacts in the BBC overseas section based in Kingsway. As well, I had a working relationship with a company in Lebanon, Baalbeck Studios. The greatest compliment ever paid to me was when, after several weeks trying to solve a problem, the general manager took a project away from his own brother in the Middle East and handed it to me.

Years later I won high praise from P&G management for spending a week in a recording studio producing Arabic translations of several American commercials. We spent endless hours trying to synchronise the Arabic with the American lip movements, and did so with a surprising degree of success using a system developed by the company De Lane Lea. My early editing skills proved a godsend and the management in Geneva could not believe what they were seeing. Of the many commercials I wrote and produced for Geneva, one in particular sticks out in my mind. It was for the launch in Africa of Tide, the washing powder as a solid bar. We built an African hut in a small studio just off Baker Street. The woman chosen to do her washing outside was a week or two later to win a TV talent competition. Her name was Patti Boulaye.

The two main competitors in the soap powder and detergent market were Procter & Gamble and Lever Brothers, the makers of Persil. From time to time, there were secret products, or a product upgrade, to be launched and, of course, keeping the details secret was vital. But when it came to casting Arabic families, and especially Arabic children, the pool in London in those days was shallow, to say the least. Nick and I had a successful session casting two brothers in a Tide commercial for the Middle East, and when Nicky questioned the mother, she revealed that the children's father ran the Persil plant in that market.

We looked at each other and resolved simply to ignore it. To do anything else would have made the situation far worse. Years later, I was to make a potentially worse mistake when I arranged to film a Fairy liquid commercial in a supermarket in Kingston. The supermarket was directly under the Head Office of Lever Brothers!

Part of my responsibility was to provide scripts to the local and international companies in the group. This meant that, in effect, I had to have a creative department. One day my secretary came in with a letter from a young man who was working as a scaffolding erector. Apparently some friends had encouraged him to look for another career. I arranged an interview and he came to see me, clearly very shy and blushing the colour of beetroot. After a brief chat, I gave him six subjects to write fifteen second commercials for. I told him not to get others to help as I would soon find out if the work was not his own. The young man returned a week later with his ideas and to my absolute surprise – and delight – five out of the six ideas could have been shot the next day, with few changes, if any.

He was clearly a first-class creative talent. So I gave him a job right there and then.

Around the same time, an advertising agency, Mather and Crowther, was preparing to launch the Triumph Herald on the cinema screens. There was intense competition between P&D and Rank to offer the best deal. The agency had written two scripts, but the client had not yet accepted either. So I asked the agency if we could submit a script to them, thinking it might be a worthy challenge for my new employee. It was a situation that could simply not happen today, but the agency agreed and I set the young man the task.

Unbelievable as it may seem, the client preferred his script. And we were asked to put it into production. Rank was understandably put out by this as they were offering a better cinema deal. So I had to go to our chairman to ensure we matched it and retained control.

We produced the commercial in Brighton. The director was freelance and the lighting cameraman, Otto

Heller, was perhaps more famous for lighting Bette Davis than cars. The story started with a businessman parking his Triumph Herald outside a hotel on the seafront. As he disappeared into the hotel, a thief appears played by Ronnie Stevens, jumps in and drives off, only to be spotted by two policemen in a police car. A chase follows along the seafront but the Herald turns quickly onto the Banjo Groyne near the pier. The police car follows but the Herald with its tight turning circle quickly exits the Groyne, while the police car has to do a three-point turn. The chase continues through a building site where the Herald easily drives over a series of kerb stones, laid out ready to be installed. The commercial ends with the car backing into a very tight parking space and the driver getting out only to be confronted by the two policemen. He has parked outside the police station.

The film was entered in the Cannes Advertising Film Festival and, wanting to ensure my new writer got the credit he deserved, I made certain his name was listed. This may not have pleased the agency, but credit where credit is due!   I later discovered that the agency creative team was headed by David Abbott, later to become a partner in the very successful London agency, Abbott Mead Vickers, now AMVBBDO.

The commercial won a first prize in the 1964 Venice Advertising Film Festival and a diploma in the New York Festival in 1965.

It was not too long before I was able to attract an award-winning director who had a good track record and an association with a company in New York that he had set up with a previous employer. I was able to promote this and very soon was producing my first American commercial for the Speidel Company of Boston. The producer from the agency was a very pleasant guy named Don Coleman and later, when I was in New York, I was invited to dinner at his home. I was something of a hit because, as I was told, they just loved my accent. I had to tell them that I was speaking English and that they were the ones with the accent. This theory never failed to cause amusement. Don had a lovely family, and I was deeply saddened when I heard some years later that he had been widowed in a tragic accident.

I soon made another commercial for Speidel, this time for the launch of a new men's aftershave, British Sterling. Not surprisingly, the script called for traditional London backgrounds and it was decided to film on the Embankment, opposite the Houses of Parliament. The product was to be carried on a silver tray by a lady in Elizabethan costume riding sidesaddle towards the camera. On the morning of the casting session, I had a visit from an agent who wanted me to consider a new model he had signed up. I suggested that she should come in for the casting session that afternoon. She did just that and got the job!

The shoot was scheduled for a Saturday on the Embankment and all permissions had been granted. However, when I was having lunch with the client on the Thursday before the shoot, I received a phone call. It was from the police inspector who had originally given us his permission. He explained that he had forgotten a London Fire Brigade Review was taking place on the Saturday of the shoot. So we had to go for another day. I should explain that the Lambeth Fire Station is on the road opposite Parliament. I asked if Sunday would be okay, and he assured me it was. I breathed a sigh of relief. As we were scheduled for weekend work in any case, I had no trouble changing the day for the crew.

On the Saturday, the Fire Brigade Review took place in constant drizzle and I was very relieved not to be shooting that particular day as I had no weather cover or insurance. Sunday morning dawned without a cloud in the sky. We had sunshine all day and finished filming in good time. Apart from the weather, I must mention the horse, that I believe, had been used on the feature film *Henry V*. He was absolutely incredible and take after take he would walk up to the camera and stop on his mark.

Who said never work with children or animals? Not me.

The commercial was the first, but certainly not the last, instance of an incredible run of luck I was to have with the weather. The commercial turned out to be a huge success, and the model was asked to go to the States for a promotional tour. As I was due to fly to New York, I was asked to take over the costume and shoes. Customs officials at JFK seemed a little concerned, so I left them to be cleared by an agent.

I believe there was some interest in the model shown by the client, or his son, but it was not returned. The product was to be launched to the sales force at a conference in Bermuda and the agency wanted to fly me down there in their private plane. I had to turn them down as I was due in London the next day. So as not to disappoint them, I did change my flight and arrived in Bermuda to be introduced to the sales force before leaving for London some five hours later.

This commercial had a sequel, but more about that later.

There were a number of other contracts with American agencies that followed and I was to go on a brief sales trip with our American colleague. The company secretary of P&D signed a contract with the American company that, to my mind, was far too generous. I eventually managed to change it. I made many trips to New York but only filmed there on two occasions, once when I worked with the local office on a Procter & Gamble product, and much later when I made a music video with The Rolling Stones at the request of their record company in London.

One of the requirements of the Pearl & Dean production company was that it had to provide basic one-minute and fifteen-second films for the salesmen to sell to local clients. The films had to be generic insofar as they needed to be capable of being adapted to include the name and address of any local trader. These ads could be for a garage, Chinese restaurant, hairdresser or literally any other local shop or business. The basic films were known as Stock Front Parts and I wrote many of them in my day.

My next production was a commercial for Sarongster ladies girdles. The spot was designed to demonstrate the extent of the movement the garment allowed. So what better than to use dancers in black leotards wearing the girdles over the top, and where better to find the dancers than at the London Palladium? And that is exactly where we shot the commercial. I was also to use dancers in some of the local films and got to know many of them, particularly a young Australian dancer who had come over to England at the age of nineteen in 1956. His name was Tom Merrifield. Today, he is a very well-known sculptor commanding fees of many thousands of pounds. He has appeared in many West End shows and notably in the feature film, *Half a Sixpence*. He worked with me on several productions and we became friends. He was living in a small house in Devereux Court off Essex Street, just off The Strand. He and his then-partner, a lady who worked for the owner of an art gallery, Nicholas Treadwell, invited my wife and I to dinner one evening. While there I noticed that he kept the red wine in the fridge! I doubt he would do that today as he has become very famous and has items in galleries all over the world. You can buy a miniature bronze for a few hundred pounds, but a life-sized example can cost well over £200,000!

Dancers were featured in another spectacular commercial for Max Factor and it was a client close to Dickie Pearl, Ernie's brother. The commercial was filmed at Shepperton Studios, and after a dance routine, the cast was to end up at the balustrade of a bridge overlooking a river created from dry ice. The opposite skyline of skyscrapers and buildings were cut outs made to match the range of Max Factor products. The production had several problems, starting with a plumber falling off a rostrum and breaking a leg. And then the agency friend of Dickie Pearl turned up and was not happy with the girls' wardrobe, saying that they looked like "a lot of hookers in Lisle Street". Not very encouraging bearing in mind they had been wardrobed in dresses they could dance in. The agency then admitted they had a dress account and that satisfied him.

The last problem was with the closing shot – the cast looking out over the river. The camera operator was taken up on a crane to look over the top of the cast and across at the skyline. He maintained it was impossible to line up the shot. I then announced I would go up on the crane, much to the sniggers of various crew. This was not the behaviour usually expected of producers, who were seldom involved in any creative decisions. The solution was simple and obvious, the buildings were cut outs, nailed to a ground row and all that had to be done was align them with the final camera position so that from the ground they appeared to be leaning inwards, but from above, they were vertical and matched the product outlines.

The producer knew his parallax!

London remained the main target in terms of increasing turnover, and that is where the bulk of the work would continue to come from. In those days, tobacco advertising was prolific. And I was to work on many brands of cigarettes and cigars. Rothmans is worth mentioning as we were commissioned to make a short film with the Army sky diving team. This meant several meetings in a smoke-laden room at their headquarters. Rothmans had sponsored a plane for the Army team, and we were to film them as they left the aircraft. On my staff I had a very good camera technician, who, over a matter of weeks, developed a wire viewfinder to fit to the top of a 16mm camera and a helmet for a skydiver to wear with an altimeter that would alert him to pull the ripcord and inflate his parachute. Several weekends were spent testing the kit at the Sywell Aerodrome near Oxford. Eventually the first sky diving footage shot during free fall was achieved. To the best of my knowledge this was the first ever such footage and I was proved right a couple of weeks later.

One wet Saturday afternoon I was watching a sports programme on the BBC, which was very unusual for me. There was coverage of a sky diving event but the cloud cover was too low and no filming could take place. Imagine my surprise when the footage we had developed for Rothmans appeared on the screen. First thing Monday morning I was onto the BBC to negotiate a royalty fee.

After all, we had developed the technique.

Another cigarette commercial is memorable for entirely different reasons. It was to be shot on location in Malta. This time I sent another producer who had recently joined the company. At one point, while the main actor was seen driving, the camera operator was taking a low-angle shot as the car came towards him. The driver misjudged the distance and hit the camera. With the operator's eye to the viewfinder, he was seriously injured. You might say why if he was looking at the scene did he not notice it, but on a wide-angle lens it would have looked much further away – until it was too late. My first concern was to get the injured man home and he was flown back to Roehampton Hospital.

My next concern was to provide some financial assistance to his family, but there were unforeseen issues. An insurance company will not allow a payout that might imply liability, so negotiations had to start. We then discovered that the producer had hired the vehicle from a garage, but had not checked the insurance cover. The car was not insured for hire and reward. The matter was eventually sorted out reasonably satisfactorily, but it led to my setting up a comprehensive insurance scheme that I was to implement in my own company.

I was still doing battle with the directors over getting the production company properly remunerated for the creative work they were doing. Put simply, the international and local company directors saw any money paid internally as lost to their screen time budget. I had a dispute with the managing director of the international company that ended with a confrontation in front of the chairman. This resulted in the man being told, in no uncertain terms, to stop interfering with my business. One of those lunches in the directors' dining room where nobody would talk to me followed, but I was getting used to them at this stage. I was not, however, prepared for what happened next.

Two weeks later the man in question suffered a massive heart attack and died. I felt very uncomfortable at his funeral at Golders Green Crematorium.

I alluded earlier to another strike situation I was soon forced to deal with. It was only five months after I rejoined the company. It arose over a question of Christmas bonuses. At this time, I had not yet been appointed to the board, although I was general manager. The directors, who were both nephews of the chairman, along with his partner's younger brother, had decided that the production company did not deserve a bonus as they were not yet in profit. Every other company in the group was to be given a bonus. This caused outrage and a strike was threatened. The cartoon unit had been closed down before I had rejoined and this time the shop steward worked under one of the directors in the local company.

I was not at all happy with my staff being victimised for something that I did not see as being their fault, and it was certainly not my way of treating loyal staff. I met with the shop steward on the day of the company party that was due to take place in the Mayfair Hotel. I assured him that I would deal with the situation and we agreed to say nothing to anyone that evening. I had a meeting with the chairman who agreed with me, and that I had set out a perfectly reasonable case. He called a board meeting for 11 am the following day, so by the time we were all at the party, the word was out and the directors suspected something was afoot. Throughout the evening, the shop steward and I exchanged furtive glances and signals to let each other know that we had disclosed nothing.

Next morning a board meeting was convened in the chairman's office. I put my case that basically asserted that junior staff should not be penalised if the management had not brought in the business. The chairman endorsed all I said and tore a strip off the directors, telling them they were not fit to be directors. Strike threat over, but you can imagine the atmosphere in the directors' dining room after that.

I was making great strides in efficiency, but a lot more needed to be done. When I rejoined, the company had a small studio in Windmill Street, right opposite the Windmill Theatre. We still had a cameraman, camera operator, and a prop buyer on staff, as well as a prop store.

All technicians were available now as freelance employees and I decided there had to be some redundancies. I closed the studio and prop store and made three members of staff redundant. It was a major breakthrough and I believe it was ultimately good for all of the redundant employees.

The previous closure of the cartoon unit had left a basement area in 38 Dover Street vacant and I was able to secure a sum from the board to equip it as a small model animation studio. The camera technician on staff and a talented rostrum cameraman formed a new unit, and within two weeks of the studio taking on the first job, it had work scheduled for six weeks ahead. The two employees were later to set up their own small studio in Soho, and I was to use it on many occasions.

At Christmas time 1965, there was a party for the children of staff. My wife came up to London with our two children, Sarah, and Jane, born in February 1964. As far as I can remember, the party went well but I was not feeling great. I was about to go down with an attack of jaundice that would keep me away from the office for about five weeks. By now I was on the board, but still had to fight off interference from the other directors. And when I eventually returned, I found that one producer had left and the directors had been interfering again.

I had had enough and told them that as the company would probably make a loss at the end of the financial year because of their interference, they would undoubtedly blame me. I was not prepared to accept it. So here I was with two children to support and about to become unemployed. I seemed to be making a habit of this!

7

ON MY OWN

As it happened, I was immediately offered a partnership and a half share in another production company, but first I had to see the chairman.

My meeting with Ernie Pearl was both cordial and unexpected when he told me they did not want to run the company without me, and suggested that I took it over with their backing. I was rather taken aback and needed time to think it over. I came to the decision that I would take a chance if they gave me a 25% shareholding. In fact, Ernie was prepared to finance my new company and take only a 25% holding for P&D.

I asked for an initial investment of £10,000 from P&D, but only ever received £5,000. I had to find an office, set up a new company and equip the new office and cutting rooms. David Lewis, the chairman's nephew and company secretary, made life as difficult as he could by sending me to New York to negotiate the company out of the contract he had entered into without my input.

Fortunately, I was able to get the contract cancelled without penalty, and on my return to London, David thanked me by demanding that I vacate my office within the next four weeks.

Ernie Pearl put a slightly different – but essentially true – spin on the split in a press release on 18 February, 1966.

"Geoffrey Forster's separation from Pearl & Dean's production life is something that had to happen and will benefit both parties," said Ernie Pearl this week. "We decided that it would be mutually better for us and Forster, for whose ability and integrity we have a high regard, to develop our respective specialities, Cinema and TV production, rather than be bogged down by the quantity of work which we are now commissioned to do. The TV business coming our way thanks to Forster's expertise might well swamp our main business. P&D backed Forster because he possesses creative and technical ability in abundance, now we must leave him to it."

I found premises at 31 Curzon Street. I had enough future business lined up to get the company off to a flying start. I agreed to one of the producers I took with me being a junior partner, his name was Norman Burrows. The company was named Forster Burrows Associates and we also formed a documentary company, FBA Productions, standing for Forster Burrows Amram.

Robert Amram was a documentary director I had met earlier and he was without a home at the time. To this day he remains a friend now living in Mexico.

We were up and running and it was only a matter of weeks before I was contacted by an agency that handled a number of P&G accounts in the UK. Word had spread from Geneva that the UK head office wanted to meet me. I remember having lunch with a P&G production supervisor in one of my favourite restaurants, the *Tiberio* in Queen Street, Mayfair and being asked "What makes you think you can start a new production company at a time like this?" "Supreme bloody optimism!" came my reply.

I was questioned as to whether I would be working for the competitor and I made it clear that I would not turn down any other work but that neither would any client's work be disclosed to a rival. In short, all jobs would remain strictly confidential. That particular meeting led to my first P&G commercial for the UK, for Flash floor cleaner, featuring the actress, Molly Weir, who was to become their spokesperson in a whole series of commercials. We wanted to add something to the look of the commercial that historically had always shown a squared black and white floor. With the art director, we decided to cut the tiles in a rather more interesting pattern. Unfortunately, my art director went down with an attack of measles, and that caused a delay that had a considerable impact on the budget. Another innovation we wanted to introduce was to shoot a wide-angle shot which had never been done before.

I should explain if you were shooting sound at this time, the camera would have to be enclosed in a soundproof box called a blimp. The blimp restricted the lenses that could be used having, as it did, a "window" through which the scene was shot. Molly Weir, the presenter, was a superb actress and every take in her performance was both word and timing perfect. With my background in a sound studio, I knew at once that we could post-sync Molly. In other words shoot with the blimp open, thereby allowing the wide-angle lens to be used, but rendering the sound useless because of camera noise. Then immediately afterwards record her voice separately. I was told later that as my client had never seen it done this way before, he was very nervous. But he need not have worried. I knew what I was doing.

That particular shoot resulted in me producing every variation of Flash commercials for many years. In fact, it led to me becoming, by far, the largest producer of commercials for P&G in London at that time, handling productions for well over a dozen brands.

Procter & Gamble was an increasingly important client, but we worked on many blue chip brands and scooped a number of international and domestic awards.

Very soon people who said they would not work with me at P&D, knocked on the door and offered their services on a commission basis. I took on one of them who had held a very senior position in a successful production company, but had declined to join me at Pearl & Dean only to discover he did not command the support in the industry he thought he had. That was a lesson that I was to remember on many occasions in the future.

FBA productions soon began to trade and Robert directed a documentary on the Swinging London scene. I put the company into a limited partnership with Ted Francis (a cousin of author Dick Francis) and Stephen

Spurrier, a young wine merchant now very exalted and living in Paris. I did not risk any of the company's cash. Filming took place in the King's Road, of course, and in various designers' studios, as well as a night club, Sybillas and Vidal Sasoon's salon. In Carnaby Street, the unit came across Sammy Davis Jr. window-shopping, and he agreed to allow us to film him. There follows a quote from the British Film Institute when they gave a retrospective screening some thirty years later.

"Robert Amram made his film debut with his 1966 paean to the delights of swinging London's groovy chicks...the dollybirds! A kaleidoscopic documentary captures the mid-sixties zeitgeist. Vidal Sasoon snips their geometric Coifs, debs do the frug at Scotts of St James's, Mick Jagger protégé, Chris Farlowe, serenades them with his number one hit."

Unfortunately, the film was completed just as the Op Art scene mutated into hippiedom, replaced overnight by the flower child. In the words of Jagger's new song, the dollybirds were instantly *Out of Time,* as was this delightful film that was lamentably shelved.

A commercial contract I had signed just before leaving Pearl & Dean was for a monthly commercial for new Dinky Toy models, and this contract continued with the new company. We built a scale model of a motorway service area in the small studio at P&D that I still had the use of. As each new model came out, we photographed a suitable background and shot sequences to be intercut with the master scenes.

The director who had worked for me at P&D had joined the new company and brought with him the American link through which he won several awards to add to those we began to win in London.

One day in the office my secretary took a call that I told her should have gone to my partner, Norman, as it was a production he was working on. The client rang back again and made it clear that he wished to talk to me. It seems he wanted me to take over the production. This presented me with a problem as my wife and I were leaving the very next day for a camping holiday in France.

The family had to go on ahead without me, and I flew out a day later to join them. The whole episode made me question what I was working for and the answer, of course, was the family. But that did not alter the fact that my employees had wives and children all dependent on my ability to attract the work.

Following the problem that Norman had with his client, I looked closely at the turnover figures for the first twelve months. The facts spoke for themselves, I had produced 86% of the turnover. There had also been an incident that I was unhappy with when the company bought a state-of-the-art tape recorder that was given to a client as a gift. The 20% shareholding I had given away was a 20% mistake. I fired my partner, who immediately started to claim an unreasonable sum for the return of the shares. Over the next two or three years there were various attempts to attend the company AGM which was held at our accountant's office in the City. Neither my ex-partner nor his representative ever arrived before we had closed the meeting immediately after the scheduled time. I changed the name of the company and also the shareholding.

Norman made one significant contribution to the company when he introduced a young secretary who was to become my P.A. for five years before departing and forging a fantastic career for herself. Take a bow, Jo Godman. She has a much higher profile in the industry than myself, and I am very proud to have been part of it in the early stages. Some years ago when she was MD of a very successful company, we met at an industry function and I was introduced to her P.A. with the words, "This man taught me all I know."

Shortly after Norman's departure, we received a rather suspicious demand for payment of an invoice for creative work. Not only had we not commissioned any work, we also had no record of it and asked for a copy of the order which was produced on the company's letterhead. Fortunately, Jo looked at it and said, "That was not typed on one of our machines." I had made sure that all typewriters in the company were identical and with the same typeface, simply in case we ever needed to produce a long document that could then be split between two machines. I put the fellow in touch with my solicitor and, believe it or not, he actually threatened him. I made sure that our receptionist always had someone with her if any stranger came in.

Not long afterwards I had occasion to visit the office on a Sunday morning as we were setting up for a shoot on a train from Paddington Station the next day – a commercial for Benson and Hedges cigarettes with the actor Victor Spinetti. I discovered that the office had been broken into, although not much seemed to have been disturbed. At about the same time, my car was broken into outside the town house that we had recently moved into in Chislehurst. Coincidence, or not?

When Norman left, he took with him an editor, Vic Vine, and they joined another rather lower-profile company. At the time, we had just completed a Babycham commercial, but had not yet delivered the required number of prints. As luck would have it, the client wanted an alteration and I called the laboratory to arrange the recut, only to be told the prints had already been delivered. Really? Apparently they had been ordered by Norman's new company. I now held the negative and made it clear that prints could only be supplied by my company. I went to see the Head of Television at the agency and explained that had we supplied the original prints, we would have replaced them at cost. But in the circumstances, we would have to charge full price. Whether or not Norman ever got paid I have no idea. But it was the last time he attempted any such move.

We were very fortunate to be asked to produce a series of commercials for Heinz soups. The campaign became known as "Souperday", which was the theme of the accompanying jingle. The campaign was a huge success and won an award for the "Best Overall Campaign" at the Creative Circle Awards 1967 and also the top category award at the Television Mail Awards the same year. The production of commercials went on unabated and by the end of 1967, I decided the time was right to give a fireworks party at our house in Chislehurst. We had moved to a new "townhouse", very modern and with not so much work for me...or so Shirley thought. We also bought an adjoining plot that had been refused planning consent.

It was perhaps a tall order to expect many of London advertising's movers and shakers to come down to suburbia on a cold, wet November evening, but they turned up in force demonstrating the high profile of the company. One hundred and fifty brave souls were greeted to a forty-foot mobile canteen, with chefs in period costume serving rib of beef and other delicacies. Awnings had been erected along a garden wall that acted as the serving counter. Braziers kept the cold at bay and the ground and first floors of our three-storey townhouse became viewing areas. We gave a pretty impressive display (£100 bought a lot of fireworks in those days), and it was the subject of much conversation among the commuters on the local station platform the next day. With my usual concern for possible problems, I had taken out insurance to cover any potential damage caused in the area. Mercifully, it was not needed.

It is interesting to note that the trade press reported that the assembled crowd consumed sixty bottles of spirits and vermouths, eight gallons of beer, and only twenty bottles of wine.

My, how times have changed.

I was soon on my way to South Africa. A contact in London had put me in touch with a local client and I was asked to produce a commercial for a locally bottled alcoholic drink, Dry Cane, and a brandy they marketed locally. It was well before the end of apartheid, and I found myself in some uncomfortable situations. I went to dinner one evening with relatives of my friend and was told off when I thanked the black waiter for clearing away my plate. On another occasion, I was taken to a white mother's home for dinner and we stopped on the way to buy a present for her housekeeper. The family was on dangerous ground as their employee was married and not supposed to be in that area. The mother explained to me that if anything happened to her, the children would want to be looked after by the housekeeper, who was essentially part of the family. The reason for stopping en route was because the mother knew the housekeeper would be upset at not being told of my visit as she wouldn't have been able to prepare something special.

The contract called for not only filming in South Africa, but also in America, Europe and North Africa. I set up the filming for the local sequences in a rooftop bar at one of the main hotels in Johannesburg, and all went well until it came to lunch. The hotel restaurant was providing a buffet lunch, and I was told the nonwhite members of my crew would be required to eat in the kitchen area. I refused to allow it and they were duly served with the rest of us. I would probably not have got away with it had the public been in the area at the time, but it was in effect a closed location.

With my responsibility to the company and its other important clients, it was not going to be possible for me to handle the other locations. As a result, I sent a young producer to Switzerland and North Africa and another unit to the Grand Canyon. The latter descended the canyon on mules and shot the rapids on the river. Not having been present on any of these locations, I cannot comment on anything but the end results. When the film of the Colorado River was processed, the laboratory, Technicolor, reported a fault with the rushes. Fortunately for all concerned, this proved not to be too serious and could be "cut round".

A greater potential problem was the fact that the producer I had sent to North Africa had not declared the equipment when leaving the location and returning to the UK. I had no knowledge of this until two years later when I was having lunch with our bank manager and he asked me if he could release the £3,000 bond he was holding pending the equipment's safe return to the UK. The problem was not helped by the fact that the original carnet had included not only the camera equipment but also stills equipment belonging to a stills photographer who accompanied the unit on the original trip.

Some of the items had been disposed of and it was thanks to a very good relationship with the accountant of Samuelsons that we were able to assemble equipment for inspection by customs at their depot.

I will never know why the customs officer did not query that some of the items' serial numbers had been added using Dymo tape! Perhaps at this point I should explain what a carnet is. Basically it is a detailed list of all the equipment being taken out of the country, and there are copies for every border that may be crossed in the course of a production. The document has to be signed in and out of each separate country, as well as back into the UK. I was to visit South Africa several more times over the years and always enjoyed my time in that beautiful, if troubled, country.

Back in London, not only was Frank Worth, the director I had brought with me from P&D, being kept busy, but I also had several freelance directors working for me. Among them were Bertie Tyrer, a very efficient but not terribly high-profile director, John Krish, Cliff Owen and others, including Anthony Harvey, a stills photographer turned director, and most importantly, Ted Kotcheff.

Our documentary company had taken off with the production of the thirty-minute film on Swinging London. Robert Amram went to the States to look for a sale for *Dolly Story* and came back some time later with an agreement to write and direct a feature film based on the youth scene in London. I was only to get involved as associate producer, a role I had to take on to safeguard Robert's contract after the American producer went to Rome as the picture got under way. I squeezed two more people into my own office, the production manager and production secretary, so that I could keep an eye on things while still producing commercials.

The film, which was eventually titled, *The Mini Mob*, featured a group of girls who decided to kidnap their ideal men and hide them away in an old house on an island in the Thames owned by an aunt. My involvement was limited, but they could not have gone into production without my company.

The American producer, Rick Herland, had a company called American Screen Arts. They had no Bank of England permission to trade in the UK, and certainly no credit. After meeting with their solicitors, Denton Hall and Bergin, I provided finance through my credit ratings, but also became their cheque signatory, so I was always able to keep the company reimbursed for any outgoings.

There was a write-up from the National Film Theatre along with an article by Clement Freud who was a member of the cast. It would take far too much space to recount the entire story of the production, but two particular problems that I was called upon to sort out deserve mention.

The featured girls were the actress girlfriend of Robert, the director, Lucille Soong, another girlfriend of the producer, Gretchen Reagan, a third actress and a newcomer that the producer and director had found working in an antique shop. A press launch party was held at the Inn on the Park Hotel, and when the news broke, the you-know-what hit the fan because of the inclusion of the newcomer. At the time, work on a commercial was a way in which an Equity ticket might be obtained. I had just made a Pepsi Cola commercial, so I wrote a contract for the girl's appearance, got her an agent and took the contract to Equity. Fortunately, nobody wanted to see the commercial that only showed hands! The agent I chose was Beryl Vertue, who was to become one of the most successful producers of TV comedy, and the girl in question was Madeline Smith.

The second problem arose from a meeting one evening in a pub between Robert and an officer from one of the guards regiments. They agreed that at the end of the film, a detachment of guards would assault the house where the captives were held. The house just happened to be on an island in the Thames at Maidenhead. Sounds simple, but I had to clear this with the War Office and find out if and how I could insure them just in case a fully-equipped soldier fell overboard from the assault craft. In the final event, all was well and the sequence was completed without incident as it was treated by the regiment as a training exercise, something I was able to do again some years later when I used the Red Berets, as the airborne troops were known, in a commercial for Timex watches.

We were fortunate to be able to keep a full order book and made commercials for everything from cake mixes to cars, and from toys to trains. Very soon our client list included many blue chip brands, including British Rail, Heinz, Kodak, Kellogg's, Cadbury, Triumph, Guinness, Gillette, Yardley, Aer Lingus, Dulux, and several Procter & Gamble brands.

Perhaps the greatest coup was to make the first ever television commercial for Marks & Spencer. I was approached by the M&S agency, Colman Prentis & Varley (CPV), and we shot the commercial in the store in Oxford.

Harry Sheppard was the client's advertising manager at the time and he did not see eye-to-eye with the creative director of the agency; they were simply two personalities poles apart. Harry was very concerned about filming interfering with the shop's trade, but the manager told me that takings that day had, in fact, been up. The outcome of the lack of communication between client and agency was that the client started to deal directly with me, a clear indication that even at this early stage of my career, I had an understanding of a client's situation, and how best to deal with it.

For the first time, I found myself working directly for a client, with the full permission of the agency, who were only too pleased to keep their client happy.

I later produced a one-minute cinema commercial for M&S entitled, "The Wool Collector", featuring an actor called Gordon Rollings. The accompanying music track was issued as a single and for many years I kept a copy. Alas, long ago lost.

I was asked to produce a commercial for Brylcreme, a men's hair preparation most famously advertised by the cricketer, Denis Compton. The spot was to promote a competition and the prize was a new car, an MGB, that had just come to the market. We filmed two or three cars at London Biggin Hill Airport, and for some reason that I forget, shot the final scene where the car drove off

leaving a large painted logo in the road in Twickenham.
I used Twickenham Studios for many projects.

I took a fancy to the car, and the very next weekend
went and bought one, as well as a convertible Triumph
Herald for Shirley. We were clearly doing well as they
were both cash purchases. Looking back some forty
years later, it is clear that the company and I personally
had a much higher profile than I realised at the time.

I was approached by an agency that would become a
major client over the next few years to quote on a group
of commercials for British Rail. They were offering me
approximately one third of the complete package that
included introducing the new Livery, and promoting
Business Travel, Sleeper Travel and Motorail, all with
regional variations. The remaining two thirds were
to be split between two other high-profile production
companies. I pointed out that savings could be made
if I handled the entire contract, and it would be better
business for the agency to keep all the eggs in one
basket. I must have put up a convincing case because the
two other companies who were in line for a share were
disappointed when I was awarded the entire contract.

I set up a composite train and arranged for it to travel
from Wood Green to Doncaster, every day for a week.
At Doncaster there was a triangle of line that enabled
us to turn the train before returning to London with the
backgrounds showing the train always travelling in the
same direction, so no loss of continuity. Every evening
the train was turned ready for the start the next day.

I am quite sure that today there would be no chance of operating the way I did on that shoot. I had a small generator installed in a guard's van and, believe it or not, a portable camping cooker and Calor Gas cylinder. I always made a point of feeding my crew as well as possible and every day I was able to provide bacon sandwiches for morning break. Lunch was picked up in Doncaster!

There were no mobile phones in those days, but I was a member of Aircall, which gave me a radio in my car. My call sign was GREY 38. On the weekend before the shoot, I got a message that there was a problem getting the generator on the train. There was nothing I could do at the time but the operator organised a forklift truck, and by the time I arrived in Wood Green, everything was sorted out, and I certainly had reason to thank Aircall.

Our week on the train went smoothly and when we finally returned to London on the Friday evening, the key crew members were picked up to be driven to Bath where we were due to film for another two days over the weekend. Why Bath? Because we were told we could have control of the mainline from Bath to London at certain times over the weekend. It was also close to some of the best railway architecture in the country, thanks to Isambard Kingdom Brunel, who built the Great Western Railway, or as it became known, "God's Wonderful Railway". Another reason was that BR was introducing a new colour livery for all its trains and only had one for us to photograph despite the fact that they wanted a shot of two trains passing each other that would be intercut with a shot of a couple enjoying dinner on the train and raising their glasses.

We needed a location where we could shoot the train passing in one direction and then wait with the camera in a fixed position until the train returned having had the engine attached to the other end. The two shots were to be put together in the laboratory using a split screen and, as both trains approached the centre of screen, we cut to the two wine glasses touching in the dining car. I had a sneaking feeling that involving a clash of glasses, the analogy was not entirely appropriate.

That was tomorrow morning, first we had to check into our hotel which seemed perfectly satisfactory, if perhaps a little old-fashioned and definitely a little too quiet for the average film crew. After an early breakfast on Saturday, we set off for our first location and our first rendezvous with our train, which was to be seen emerging from Brunel's Box Tunnel. The shot was to start on a signal light that was almost at ground level, and as the director lined up the shot, the assistant brought the train slowly forward. The assistant was heard to shout to the driver, "STOP! STOP! YOU'VE COME TOO FAR!" Whereupon the driver leaned out of his cab and said somewhat sternly, "This is six-hundred tonnes of train, not a f...ing wheelbarrow," which put the assistant firmly in his place and relieved any tension there may have been in the crew.

The next location was the disused station at Bathampton, where we were to illustrate a new shortcut between Birmingham and the West Country. What the director intended was to use a very wide-angle 9.8mm lens and have it travel along just above the rail as it took off on a branch line. I should have told the director that his shot would be dramatic, but would not show the turn off as clearly as if it had been shot from a high angle. We had a plate layer's trolley on which to mount the camera and our operator, probably the oldest member of the crew, had to be strapped down to steady the camera which otherwise would have vibrated, making the shot unusable.

The next problem was to push the trolley, with its load, along the rails. The unit was divided into pairs that would push, each pair catching up with the trolley after it had passed them.

The first two pairs worked well, a bridge concealing the second pair, but it fell to me and the director to take over the last lap as the trolley went round the branch line. It was winter and everything had been tested, but we were now in danger of losing the light. So it was vital the trolley did not stop. We were all dressed for the cold, the director looking like the Michelin Man, while I was wearing boots, sweater and a sheepskin jacket. One tends to think of railway sleepers as being equally spaced. WRONG. They can vary considerably and if you are trying to run while pushing something only eighteen inches high and unable to see your feet, it is not an experience I would recommend. To add to our discomfort, signal cables and the points had to be negotiated. My director fell flat, leaving me as the only pusher. If I did not complete the shot, it would be too dark for another take. I was struggling and ran out of my boots, but with a final effort the trolley rolled away from me around the bend.

I nursed my sore feet and retrieved my boots as the trolley with camera and human cargo seemed to pick up speed as it moved away from me. We, of course, had a representative of BR with us, but what he had not told us was that once round the bend, there was a downward gradient and this had now taken over, camera and operator travelling under their own steam, to coin a phrase. Imagine, if you will, a middle-aged man, lying prostrate on a trolley, with sole responsibility for a very expensive camera, and an even more expensive production, which being a true professional he took very seriously. He did not dare move until he was absolutely certain the shot was "in the can", at which point he told the assistant he assumed was behind him to, "Cut the camera." Nothing happened. Again he repeated his request to turn the camera off, again no response. Gathering pace in the increasing gloom, he finally, taking care not to move the camera, managed to turn his head sufficiently to see that he was completely alone. With admirable presence of mind, he got his left foot on a wheel and, with the aid of a piece of wood on the trolley, managed to stop the trolley just in time before he would have made dramatic contact with a level crossing gate.

That evening, having relived the day's events in the bar, we were in a suitably mellow and rather light-headed mood when we went into dinner in the hotel dining room. Still laughing at the day's events, we were confronted by a female string trio. They brought to mind Noel Coward's phrase in another story closely linked to trains, "There should be a society for the prevention of cruelty to musical instruments." As you can imagine, our mood and the surroundings made us perhaps rather too noisy for some of the older guests. I am sure that had they been aware of the events of the day, they would have joined in our laughter. However, there were no complaints, and we retired to prepare for an early call the next day.

Sunday morning dawned cold, with a light dusting of snow. By 8 am, we were on our first location in a field outside Bath where we set up to shoot the two scenes of our liveried train travelling in each direction.

The railway line was some six hundred yards away, on the other side of a canal. Behind us were the gardens of houses backing onto the field. So here we were, a group of people standing in a snow-covered field some six hundred yards from the railway line, when a man in dressing gown and overcoat peered over the fence at the bottom of his garden and asked us what we were doing there. The assistant director promptly gave the truthful answer, "Waiting for a train." The poor fellow went back to bed rather confused.

The contract with British Rail continued with two further commercials. The first was for Motorail, and involved loading a train with some forty or fifty cars and setting off for a rural location in the Cotswolds. The other was for business travel between Edinburgh and London. They were two separate shoots, linked by one thing – food. It may seem as though I am always thinking about where my next meal is coming from, but whoever it was that said, "An army marches on its stomach," could very well have been talking about a film crew.

I should mention at this point that the cameraman I had employed for the Motorail shoot, was a Frenchman, Patrice Pouget. I had worked with him on one or two occasions and he was to photograph the train from a helicopter. He was very experienced, and with a partner, had made the well-known feature film *A Man and a Woman*, which I am ashamed to say I never saw. Some years later, Patrice was killed in a light plane crash. He was a great loss.

A well-fed unit is a happy unit and will work above and beyond the call of duty for the producer who looks after them. It has always been a priority as far as I am concerned to provide the best catering possible for my crew, and not only that, but to ensure that if agency or client representatives are on the shoot, they are not treated any differently than the technicians. In the early days, there was a tendency on the part of some agencies to organise special wines in a caravan during the lunch break.

So what part did food play on our Motorail commercial location?

The necessary cars were hired from a rental company in the West of London and loaded onto the train in the sidings at Olympia. The unit travelled by road to the Cotswolds, and checked into their hotel before the next morning's rendezvous with the train and the helicopter from which our cameraman would be filming the train as it travelled through the picturesque countryside. On the first day, I had arranged for packed lunches to be prepared at the hotel as we were told there were no other facilities available, and we had no idea where the train might stop at lunchtime. The food was perfectly acceptable, but I soon discovered that our train had been made up to look as normal a service as possible. So it had a fully-equipped dining car complete with kitchen. I checked and found that gas and water supplies were connected. It was a challenge that could not to be resisted.

Next time we stopped, I made straight for the nearest telephone box and called my office in London. We had a driver ready to take the day's film to the laboratory, collect it again at 6 am, and bring it back to the train where we had an editing machine and could see the rushes. I briefed the ever-reliable Jo to go shopping for various items and arranged for her to be picked up at 5.30 am the next morning, collect the rushes on the way and join me on the train. That day we served not only the obligatory bacon and egg rolls, but also a three-course lunch with a choice of main course, much to the delight of the unit. Where there's a will, there's a way!

The commercial for business travel from Edinburgh to London was set up as a race between a rally driver and a couple travelling by train. We had already covered the interior shots of the couple, but they had to come to Edinburgh with us to cover the start of the race at the Forth Bridge car park. The official start was set up, complete with banner and a small crowd of onlookers.

It was winter and very cold, but fortunately there was a restaurant in the car park and we were all able to have a good mid-morning break before moving to our next location, which was on Forestry Commission land at Peebles.

In those days I carried with me an insulated urn and a supply of polystyrene cups, and as lunch was likely to be at least a moveable feast, I filled the urn with good, hot Scotch broth. We had two large limos, a camera car, an equipment truck, and the two action cars, one for the rally driver and a second in which the couple had headed off towards Edinburgh station. The forest track we were using rose sharply from a car park on the main road. We parked the limos, the action car and camera car and disappeared up the snow-covered track. I drove up and dispensed hot broth to any crewmember who came my way.

We were due to return to London that evening and shoot the arrival scene at Euston the next morning. To keep the costs to a minimum, I was to take the overnight train, while the crew was to fly back. I arranged for a slap-up dinner for the crew on arrival back at the hotel before everyone had to leave for the airport. Once filming in the forest had finished, we still had some car-to-car shots to cover on the journey back into town. Intercut with the forest shots, they would contrast with the previously completed shots of the couple enjoying a leisurely dinner on the train.

When we reassembled in the car park to set up for the return journey, I was more than a little surprised to find one of our limos missing. A young assistant from the agency, who was working for me as a trainee at the time, told me that the account executive had taken it and the young actress playing the part of the train passenger to the local hotel for tea. I was furious at the thoughtlessness of his action in the face of a team working for him in blizzard conditions without proper food. Matters were made worse when the assistant said he would take the other limo to find them, a move I immediately vetoed. We squeezed everyone into the remaining cars and set off to shoot our road scenes, car-to-car.

Halfway back we stopped to reload the camera, and change from one car to the other. As we sorted ourselves out, I noticed the second limo pull up on the end of our convoy. I stormed back to the car, pulled open the door and gave the account executive a lesson in how to behave when people were working for him under extreme conditions. The actress with him looked on in amazement as I gave him a piece of my mind and slammed the door shut. Apparently she turned to him and said, "Aren't you *his* client?" to which he replied, "Yes, but Geoff knows me very well." Next morning, the arrival was filmed on the forecourt of Euston Station and, surprise, surprise, the couple on the train were there refreshed and relaxed when the exhausted driver finally pulled in.

The history of the company reflects the development of the industry as a whole in those relatively early days. I took on a young Colin Frewin as a producer, and later when the company he was working for, MRM, went bust, I took on his older brother, Michael, as a director

115

and changed the name of the company to Forster Frewin and Partners.

The Austin 1100 was launched with the revolutionary hydrolastic suspension. This was a new form of suspension, and a commercial was needed to illustrate it. The script came to us and was very specific, calling for the car to be driven through London past various landmarks. Simple you might say, but the catch was the camera had to be under the car to show the new suspension, which had been highlighted in different colours.

These were very early days and there were no very low trailers that would become available in later years, so there were two problems. We had to mount the car on a steel frame on a low loader and then make provision to be able to turn the wheels as the car drove around. That was hard enough but the crew, lights and camera had to be accommodated as well. The second obvious problem was where were we going to be able to film it? It was clearly going to have to be on a Sunday when the streets would be clear enough to allow our unwieldy, large vehicle to drive past some very impressive locations. I went to see the City of London Police, and got the permission we needed. A big problem was that the car was, by now, quite high off the ground, and it was not easy to make the shots look convincing.

Filming went well during the morning, and we covered much of the City including St Paul's Cathedral, the Law Courts and Tower Bridge before it was time for lunch. We had caterers with us and had sent them on ahead as we left the City and proceeded down The

Strand. We parked up on Horse Guards Parade, which, of course, is a Royal Park. And it was not long before we were moved onto a side street off Whitehall, where the caterers had already set up.

That was all well and good, but our cameraman had been in urgent need of a comfort break, and had descended from the low loader and headed off to find the nearest facility. No one saw him go, and when feeling rather relieved, he returned to Horse Guards Parade, only to find there was no one there. It took him almost three quarters of an hour to find us in a cab that had a rather hefty fare on the meter.

Among our numerous awards was one for Watneys for a series featuring Peter Cook and Dudley Moore in their well-known TV personas as E.L. Wistey and partner sitting at a table in a pub. One of the scripts was a take-off of the then-current detergent campaign, the White Tide Man, who would visit housewives and give them either five pounds if they had the product or ten pounds if they had a large pack.

I am not sure whether it was simply an agency script, or whether Peter had some influence over it, but what he delivered was, "Look out for the Watneys Brown man, and if you can't show him a bottle, he will stamp on your glasses and take five pounds away from you." I doubt very much that that version ever went on air.

A spot for the Triumph Herald became yet another award winner, in both the UK and the U.S.

Most unusually, a commercial we made for Ajax floor cleaning liquid won an award. It came about because the selling line for the product was, "Makes floors too clean to walk on." The commercial started with a housewife opening her front door to a friend, before proceeding to walk down the hall on the walls. The set had to be rigidly constructed so that it could be literally turned on its side. All the set dressings had to be secured and drapes held firmly in place, while the ladies coats had to be made to look as though they were reacting to the effects gravity. Today, it would all be simple trickery, but we had to shoot it for real, and that is why we got the award.

There was one company in particular I regarded as a challenge, James Garrett and Partners, who were just about the largest and most successful production house at the time. One of my regular clients once said to me, "If you were to join him, you would be unbeatable."

Garretts had an office in Johannesburg, but did not enjoy a great reputation at the time. I had already established a relationship with a client in South Africa and when I took a call from the client at lunch in a local restaurant, I said that I would get one of my producers down there the next day, and I did, and it resulted in our getting the contract from under the nose of Garretts local office. The contract was for Caltex, the petrol giant, and we made a space-themed commercial in the UK for Caltex Boron.

The next contest was much nearer home and was for the UK launch of a new car from Rootes. I should mention at this stage the importance of the quote letter that the producer sends to the agency. It is vital that any inclusions – or exclusions – are specified and the importance of the letter is best illustrated by this particular contract. The script called for a plane to be seen landing at an airport and greeted by a pack of reporters and photographers. A glamorous blonde film star comes down the steps but the reporters rush to the front of the plane which opens to reveal a car that then is driven down a ramp onto the tarmac, whereupon it is immediately surrounded. The film star walks off in disgust as the camera literally caresses the car. The first and most important requirement was to find a car-carrying aircraft, and within a few days we had located all the possible planes in Europe and North America.

We were, as I said, in competition for the project and discovered that rather than sending the crew to the location by scheduled flights, the other company was proposing to put them on the plane with the car. By budgeting that way, we were able to come up with a better price and secure the contract. The plane we decided on was a Carvair based at Southend Airport that had the capacity to take four cars and some twenty or so passengers. We decided to shoot in Majorca where we were able to negotiate a deal with Palma Airport, as it was December and not the holiday season. The main problem was that the agency wanted the car to drive off the plane, whereas it would normally have been unloaded by hydraulic lift as the nose of the plane through which the car would exit was eleven feet six inches above ground, and once the car was out, the suspension of the plane would take it up a further eighteen inches.

The problem was solved by designing a lightweight ramp in sections that could be carried in the aircraft and assembled on location for the car to drive down. After some discussion and exchange of technical information, our insurers were satisfied and provided the necessary cover and we were all set to go. To save weight, the ramp had been constructed as a steel frame with two six-inch aluminium channels to take the wheels. The crucial dimensions were supplied by the agency as we had not been able to see the car. Construction was due to be completed by the Friday for delivery to Southend, and then loaded on the plane before the departure scheduled for the Sunday.

The director, the agency and myself were already in Majorca scouting for locations and driving shots, and on the Saturday I sent a young assistant from my office to check that the ramp was ready. He thought that it looked too wide for a relatively small car and, fortunately for us all, especially the agency, he had the presence of mind to contact the customs warehouse where the car was being held under wraps and ask them to measure the track width. Surely enough, we had been given the wrong dimensions and the engineering company had to work overnight to cut the ramp which was made in three sections and welded it back together several inches narrower in time to get it to the airport on the Sunday morning. The young man showed great common sense and initiative and later became an accomplished feature producer.

The requirement for the agency to provide us with the dimensions was specified in the bid letter and the consequences had we not discovered the fault do not bear thinking about. We had worked on a number of car commercials and another crucial point that I made in the bid letter was that we must have cars with light-coloured interior trim, as we knew from experience that you would not be able to see sufficient detail if the interior was dark. We were provided with two cars with black interiors and were told that they were the only two available from the factory. Once again, I thanked my lucky stars that I had written such an explicit letter.

Our plane had been hired for a week and had to leave on the Friday, but we were still in need of some more driving shots and stayed on an extra day. I was very fortunate in finding a British Airways plane that had come out with holidaymakers for Christmas and was due to fly back to London later that day empty. Back in London the film was edited and the agency demanded still more driving material. Unbelievably, they produced a storyboard that was dated two days after we had left and was different to the one we had quoted on. It was clearly the result of further thoughts on the part of the client. The post-dated storyboard demonstrated yet again the staggering incompetence of the agency. I sent a camera crew back to Majorca where the cars were being stored pending a stills shoot. The additional material was shot and added to the cut.

It seems that the client was yet to see the film and when it was eventually shown to him it was no surprise to me to be told that we had to reshoot the interior shots with light-coloured interior trim. We had all been sworn to secrecy about the name of the car. In fact, the contract and all documentation referred to Rootes B car, so when I set up a further shoot at the RAF station West Malling in Kent, I was shocked to see two cars delivered by transporter with the logo in full view of anyone, including our crowd of forty extras.

Why the secrecy? The name of the car was the Avenger, and the name and theme tune were taken from the enormously popular television series of that name. I cannot explain why, but change after change was demanded by the client, who was pushing claims for the vehicle further than he could hope to justify. The result was that with a budgeted, and confirmed, three-hour recording and dubbing allowance, we ended up with twenty-nine and a half hours – but again not at our expense.

All in all there could not have been a better demonstration of the importance of a comprehensive bid letter.

There is a saying common in filming circles that, "It doesn't count on location," a phrase used to justify, or excuse, some of the many romantic liaisons that are part and parcel of men and women living and working together in close proximity away from home. There was a classic illustration on the shoot in Majorca that I have just described.

As I said, we had to stay on an extra day to cover more driving shots but makeup, wardrobe and sound were not needed and it gave them free time for sightseeing before the late afternoon flight back to London. As usual at the end of the schedule on the Friday evening many of us ended up in a rather noisy bar in the centre of Palma. As the evening wore on, I was approached by the owner of the bar who clearly knew that I was with the film unit. He asked me if I would talk to a German film director who was in need of some assistance. The director in question was accompanied by a six-foot blond actor who could not have been more than thirty years old, and that was his problem. He had to transform the actor into an ageing Don Quixote for a shoot at dawn, and he had no makeup artist. The request was a simple one. He had discovered that our makeup artist was free the next morning and asked if she could help him. You may be thinking that this was a practical joke as I did but after some time I realised that the request was genuine, if rather bizarre.

I had no objection in principle, but made it clear that it would be entirely up to the lady as it meant getting up at 3.30 in the morning. He agreed to pay whatever she wanted to do the job and so I agreed to phone the hotel. It was eleven o'clock at night and the bar was full, to make matters worse when the barman gave me the phone it was in a corner next to the jukebox. Having established with the night porter that the lady in question was in her room, it took some time to get her to answer the phone and the conversation that followed would have made a comedy script on its own. She had clearly been asleep and had woken to hear me in a crowded bar offering her employment in a few hours time at whatever she liked to charge. Needless to say, I was not taken seriously and she eventually gave up and left the negotiations to me.

Would anyone, I asked myself, believe such an unlikely story when practical jokes among the crew were not that uncommon? I realised that I was going to have to stay with it and be there when the Germans arrived at the hotel at 3.30 am. I met them in reception and asked the porter to call the lady's room. There was no reply, but eventually I found myself talking to a rather bemused lady who was quite possibly drunk. I had to tell her that she would find out it was not a joke when she sobered up.

I set off for her room leaving the three Germans in reception. The sight that greeted me when she slowly opened the door was not a pretty one. The empty bottles and remains of dinner told their own story. The lady had clearly had a visitor and was not expecting another one. I explained, as gently as possible, that the two Germans were in reception and that she had agreed to do the makeup. Faced with the reality of the situation, she insisted that I did not leave her and after organising copious cups of black coffee, and trying to bring some degree of order back to the room, I became for the first time in my life a makeup assistant. The director and his actor arrived in the room, I have already said that the actor was young and blond, now he had to be transformed into a bearded old man by a makeup artiste who could barely stand, let alone see.

As if it were not enough, he arrived clutching a plastic bag containing a stage wig and beard, both of which had been sprayed with silver paint and accordingly set into a solid mass. My role became that of hairdresser that involved trying to comb out the offending hairpieces so that they could be glued into place. Eventually the job was done, and my opinion on the makeup was sought. I pointed out the age lines on the left of his face would be better if they matched those on the right. That done our new found friends departed with a bottle of spirit gum and a couple of spare, combed out, hairpieces.

I have absolutely no idea what or why the Germans were filming but assumed it had to be something amateur and finding a professional unit had been a chance not to be missed. I was soon to find out why our makeup lady had been so ill-prepared. Another crew member, who was in the know, told me that the lady in question had enjoyed a relationship with someone who I just happened to have booked on our crew, and that he had chosen that night to end the affair.

Next day I was given a present of a leather tie! One occasion when it obviously did count on location!

It has always been a principle of mine to be completely honest with any location owner in advance and try to ensure they do not get a nasty shock when the crew arrives. Only too often I have been aware of someone's dismay when they have not been properly briefed and were expecting a cameraman and a couple of assistants. Fortunately, those days are in the past and television itself has played a part in educating people.

I say that I always told the truth and that is correct, but I do remember one or two instances where I had to be a little economical with the details. The first occasion was in a commercial for the Triumph Herald car. It was a very good script involving a young male driver who spots an attractive blonde and does an immediate U-turn to illustrate the car's turning circle. Unfortunately, the girl turns down a flight of steps followed, of course, by our driver, to demonstrate the suspension. On reaching the bottom of the steps, the lady is greeted by her boyfriend and they embrace. Seeing that he is on a losing wicket, our hero immediately reverses back up the steps. The final line of the voiceover was, "The most go anywhere car in its class".

I spent a weekend scouring London for a suitable flight of steps. The steps had to be sufficiently long for the required action, and not too steep. There was only one location that would satisfy all our requirements, the steps at the rear of the Royal Albert Hall in Kensington. Although the road around the back of the Albert Hall was a public road, there was no through traffic so it was ideal for the U-turn and the steps were shallow leading down to the street below. I discovered that the steps were owned by the landlord of the flats that bordered them, Albert Court.

Without any alternative location, and I had really tried everywhere, I had to gain permission. I approached the company and negotiated a fee for the use of the steps for photography. It was the truth. I had just omitted the prefix "Cine".

Once filming started complaints started to come in from local residents but possession is, as they say, nine-tenths the law, and I was confident that I could keep things going until we finished. Several phone calls and an indemnity letter later and I had agreement to film until 2 pm. As it was, we finished unmolested at 5 pm.

The commercial won awards both here and in America.

Another occasion was many years later and rather more complicated. There was a minor scandal involving a parliamentary researcher who was accused of involvement with an MP and a senior journalist. The woman concerned fled the country. At the time I was producing almost weekly commercials for the *Daily Mail*, and after filming one day, I was telephoned by the head of television at the agency and asked to see her when we wrapped. Once there I was sworn to secrecy and became one of only four people outside the newspaper to know that they had found the lady and brought her back to the UK and were keeping her in a safe house. Wanting to capitalise on this major scoop, the paper needed a commercial, but it had to be shot in secret and I was being handed the problem.

Booking the crew without telling them what they were filming was no problem, but what about the location and, even worse, the wardrobe? I had a regular wardrobe mistress working for me at the time and I briefed her and sent her out in a car with a telephone (No mobiles, then). I suggested that her subject would likely be a size ten, which I thought was a reasonably safe bet and said I would phone her if I got any more information. She was to supply a complete wardrobe for a country weekend, lingerie, business clothes, cocktail dress and riding wear, in fact, the lot, as the location would be a classic English country house.

My job was to find a location and convince the owner to allow me to film without knowing what the subject was. Starting close to home, I approached a certain Viscount, but I think he suspected the truth, or maybe he thought I was making a pornographic film! Eventually I was put in touch with a small country house with an estate north of London. The owner of the house was the widow of an Earl, and she lived there with her second husband and they were hoping to develop a conference business, which played nicely into my hands. Having agreed a fee I made sure to get the cheque to them as fast as possible on the assumption that if they had accepted payment, it would be difficult to withdraw from the agreement. I called the crew to a North London studio and then sent them off to rendezvous at a certain junction on the M1. I would then lead them to the location.

On our arrival, I discovered that the lady had been kept in a house very near to where I was living in Sussex. Maybe I should have pressed for my first choice rather harder, but hindsight is a great advantage. Filming was slow to start and the lady was hard to please, and was certainly not the accomplished rider she had claimed to be. We had a very docile horse for her but she was clearly scared of him and it became difficult to make her appear convincing. While all this was going on, I was approached by the estate manager, who had put two and two together and worked out what we were doing. He had apparently informed his employer who was, I believe, in the legal profession. No objection was raised, but just to be on the safe side I suggested that the manager should check the background of the scenes to ensure nothing that identified the house could be seen.

Filming was eventually completed, but the client wanted some more sound interviews and the last members of the crew did not to leave until almost 11 pm! During the day we had become aware of a couple of photographers peering over hedges on the estate with long lenses pointed in our direction. No one on my crew had any information about the job or location, so we assumed there must have been a leak, either intentionally or otherwise, from the paper.

The film was edited, it had been a difficult production, but worse was to come. Screening was scheduled for the Saturday and Sunday...and that Saturday was the day of the Hillsborough disaster.

As a result, the commercial was never seen.

From the very earliest days, music has been an important part of the soundtrack of many commercials. During my time at Pearl & Dean, it was towards the end of the big band era and I had had visits from one or two of the bandleaders of the day putting themselves forward in the hope of getting a commission to compose a track for a commercial. It was not, of course, my job as producer to commission music. That was the agency's responsibility. I remember clearly Roy Fox as being the first to approach me towards the end of a very successful career in America, Australia and England.

It will be for others to write the history of music in commercials, so I will just mention one or two of the musicians I worked with. Joe Roncoroni was a larger-than-life character who, along with Ken Jones, were to become both publishers and producers of the Zombies. John and Joan Shakespeare were a husband and wife team. John had formed the group, The Ivy League, but became better known for composing the theme tune to the very successful television programme, *Terry and June*. Cliff Adams formed the group The Star Gazers in 1950, and joined the BBC show band in 1954. He was to go on to have the very popular radio programme, *Sing Something Simple*.

When it came to jingles, perhaps the most prolific composer in the 1960s was Johnny Johnston. Johnny composed the jingles for several commercials that I produced. Most notably for 1001 carpet cleaner with the line "Cleans a big carpet for less than half a crown". I produced many commercials for Fairy liquid using the lines, which I am sure many will remember, "Now hands that do dishes can feel soft as your face with mild green Fairy liquid". That jingle alone must have made him a fortune as it was run for so many years.

Johnny was approached by the BBC in 1948 to form a close harmony group and compose the signature tune for a new radio programme they were about to launch. Johnny formed a group called The Keynotes and the programme was *Take It from Here*. The rest, as they say, is history. The most memorable jingle Johnny wrote for any of my productions was the one for the "It's Heinz

Souperday" series of soup commercials. Johnny and his wife Nona retired to Geneva in Switzerland, where I was able to visit them many times.

Not all music is specially composed and I am sure we can all recall many classical pieces that have been adapted over the years, British Airways and Benson & Hedges come readily to mind. There have also been a number of commercials that have profited from buying the rights to a successful song or theme tune. The Avenger commercial I produced being a case in point. It is very seldom that musicians are seen in vision, certainly in the past it was likely to be due to opposition from the musicians union, but there was one occasion when I employed part of the London Symphony Orchestra. The commercial was for a detergent. I do not recall the script in any detail, but there was a question as to what piece of classical music they would play at the start of the commercial.

As we needed instant recognition, I suggested that there was only one suitable piece – the opening four notes of Beethoven's Symphony No. 5. Those four notes had become the symbol of victory during the last war. It was agreed and when filming went ahead I noticed that all except one of the violinists were showing a neat white cuff below the sleeves of their tailcoats. I politely asked if he could pull his down, only for him to reveal that he was wearing only a shirtfront with no sleeves attached.

I guess you can't win them all!

Detergent and soap powder advertising may not lead to the most exciting of filming projects, but it has provided a lot of work for a lot of people over the years. And has certainly provided the odd moment or two of amusement. In the sixties, testimony from the public was very popular and was used to advertise many brands.

I have worked on testimonials from housewives who were given dishwashing liquid with a window in the pack so that the amount used over a given period could be seen. I was filming outside Cambridge on one particular occasion and was going ahead of the unit to warn the lady of the house when we would be arriving to interview her. On one doorstep I was talking to a young child who had opened the door and said, "I don't expect mummy is used to seeing strange men in the afternoon," or words to that effect. "No such luck," said mum, who had just appeared. I was rescued by the arrival of the camera crew. Today I could certainly not have that conversation.

On one occasion we were shooting a testimonial with a well-known TV presenter interviewing a housewife and acting as presenter. When we broke for afternoon tea, the presenter disappeared into the house with the makeup artist and carried on a conversation completely unaware that she was still wearing her radio mic. She emerged rather red-faced. I also covered testimony for a fabric softener shot in Bognor when the testimonees were found by a hidden camera picking up those who purchased the product in a store but, most of the testimonials that I was to work on were for a major brand of detergent.

We set up hidden cameras in a variety of locations and on one occasion set up in a Civic Centre, where a ballet company was due to appear very soon. This gave us the perfect opportunity to conceal our three cameras, one focusing on the washing, one on the whole scene and the last a close-up on the lady. What we had set up was a ballet practice room complete with bar and large mirror. We had put up a false wall and the mirror – which was two-way – concealed the cameras in a darkened room behind it.

At the time I had a house where I was able to store props and the mirror was returned to me. When we moved house some years later, it was still stored, and not knowing what to do with it, it became a rather unusual gratuity to some bemused removal men.

It is a sad reflection on today's society that if I were to go about finding locations for a series of detergent commercials that I was contracted to make as I did in the 1960s, I would almost certainly be arrested, and probably charged. The commercials were to feature local housewives who would bring their dirty washing to a stand – rather like an exhibition stand – that we would have set up in an open area such as a green or recreation ground. How did we select our location? The objective of the commercial was to get testimony from the housewives and we were looking for ladies we thought would not be camera-shy. They would have to be real mums as they would have the biggest washing challenge. Usually the mums would be found by a research team, but we were looking for our subjects before we could decide the location.

With a representative of the client with me, we would park near school gates to see the mums as they collected their offspring. It is perhaps worth mentioning that, at the time, I was driving a Lotus! A research team would then recruit housewives once we had agreed the location. We discovered, through experience, country towns, and, in particular, cathedral cities were where we were most likely to get the best testimony. On one recce I stopped outside Salisbury to check our map. By chance rather than design, I stopped in a lay-by opposite an AA kiosk. Having satisfied ourselves about the next stage of our route, we started off again. Or rather tried to. The car would not start. After some time, an AA man managed to get us going, but could not pinpoint the fault. Later that afternoon we found a garage with an electrician and pulled in to have the car checked again. After a relatively short time, he asked me if I had a secret cut out switch. I had and had accidentally activated it when putting the map back in the glove box.

We filmed in Winchester, Salisbury and Chichester before the client announced he wanted more regional accents, and directed us to find a location further North. We ended up selecting Northampton, a much more industrial area and we were not confident and so it turned out. We set up on a communal area in the centre of a large council estate. The weather was against us, and we decided to film inside an Air House, which was essentially a huge tent kept up by air pressure provided by large pumps.

After the first shoot in the series, when my director said we should start with a shot of a housewife coming down the road behind our stand, I realised that the last thing we needed was a director who wanted to make a creative contribution – when all you are interested in is what the housewives are saying. From that point on, every commercial was directed by my agency producer.

Filming is unpredictable at the best of times, and schedules get stretched. On day two in Northampton, in the late afternoon, the ladies banded together and demanded more money than we had agreed to pay them. Payment to anyone giving testimony has always been strictly controlled and should be restricted to expenses or loss of earnings. The ladies of Northampton had decided they wanted more. Fortunately, I had a senior client with me. If we could not continue, the whole commercial could have been rendered pointless. Our client reached an agreement and we were able to complete, but it was never going to be as satisfactory as in the past.

I mentioned that we had filmed in Salisbury, and I had the same senior client on that location with me. The commercials showed ladies bringing their dirty washing to our stand, and then returning the next morning to retrieve their now sparkling washing.

After dinner at our hotel we would always visit the team of locally recruited women who would wash and iron the laundry overnight. On this occasion, my client, a tall rugby playing South African said, "Aren't we near Stonehenge?" "Yes," I said. "Would you like to see it? I'll drive you down there after dinner." He accepted my invitation, and after a good dinner we set off. We arrived at the site and stood looking over the barbed wire fence some considerable distance from the stones. "I wish we could get closer," bemoaned the client. "Why not," I said, probably reacting to the wine we had both enjoyed at dinner. We climbed the fence and walked into the centre of the circle. It was awe-inspiring to stand there in the moonlight without tourists, and the client was suitably impressed.

As he stood in front of one of the arches he raised his hands to indicate his amazement at its impressive size. As he did so, we were suddenly bathed in light and I found myself wondering how a car with such bright headlights could possibly be in what I knew to be a field. "Was that me?" asked the client, rather sheepishly. "I'm afraid it must have been," I said and we agreed to walk, rather quickly, back to the fence and make our escape. We got back over the fence just in time as a security guard, with a rather large dog, emerged from the access tunnel.

The client returned to the hotel pleased to have seen Stonehenge and in the clear knowledge that it had been ALL LIGHT ON THE NIGHT.

As time went on, I started to think that I might some day need someone to manage the company leaving me free to concentrate on getting new business. One of my advertising agency clients was J. Walter Thompson, and one of the administrators of their television department was Denis Singleton, who I would very much have liked to employ on his retirement. His daughter was the well-known children's television presenter, Valerie Singleton.

One of my other clients had his own ideas about the company. I was filming at Halliford Studios near Shepperton, and was in the middle of a hectic week of filming. He wanted me to go to dinner with him and his wife in Highgate the next day. To say that it was inconvenient is an understatement. I went despite the fact that I was working early mornings and had a very full day. Over dinner he suddenly said to me, "I thought I might be the Managing Director of your company." I was speechless, as anyone I was less likely to employ I could not imagine.

As a result of some successful American productions, I was approached to set up a creative hot shop in the Black Forest in Germany being proposed by Interpublic, at the time the largest international group of agencies.

Not necessarily in the correct order here are some of the other requests I had.

I was asked by the MD of an agency to meet with a colleague who wanted to invest in production. I had to explain that I did not need an investment, and that production was a very personal business, not something that could be costed and turned out on a production line. A similar approach came from Peter Peck, a studio owner who had a very successful business in the stills catalogue market.   Having refused his offer, he turned his attention to another company, Wynne Films, and asked me if I could run it if he managed to buy it. Wynne was a long-established company run by Derek Wynne originally in Brighton but recently moved to a studio in

Charlotte Street. I said yes, I could, but strongly advised him against buying the business. I had lunch with a producer I knew who had worked for Wynne to find out some background and repeated my advice.

Shortly afterwards, I heard that Peter had in fact bought the company – against my advice. I believe it cost him dear when it went into liquidation.

Some time later, I was introduced to an American, who again wanted to expand the business. He had been in contact with two brothers who had inherited a cinema business in the North, possibly Leeds. They wanted to tie up with me and form a new enterprise and there was sustained pressure from the American who I had in my office. He had the very irritating phrase, "Pretty as a speckled pup under a red wagon." I had to keep him at arms length and refused to make any changes to the company, although I did pay his membership fees to a golf club. After a lunch with the brothers, a breakfast meeting was arranged with their solicitor, Lord Goodman, at his apartment in Mayfair.

I say a breakfast meeting but it was more a question of watching him eat. We were not even offered coffee! I had heard rumours about why he was in London. So arranged a meeting at the American Embassy to check on him. At the interview I said that I knew that they would not disclose information on a U.S. citizen, but would they answer a question? They said they would and I found out that he may not have been welcome in certain states, I think divorce had something to do with it. It was also apparent that although a deal with the brothers was attractive, it was clearly going to be an uphill struggle to gain any degree of control. That put an end to that particular American dream!

Most companies I was asked to help, or take over, were in financial difficulty. I was approached to take over Cammel Hudson, a rather high-profile company. The partners were David Cammel and Hugh Hudson, who went on to direct *Greystoke* and *Revolution*. The company was in need of cash, so again, after a good dinner in Chelsea, the answer was no. The next approach was rather simpler and more interesting. It came from comedian, Bob Monkhouse. Bob had a company in partnership with Malcolm Mitchell called Mitchell Monkhouse, and had their offices above a club, the Pair of Shoes in Hertford Street, beside the Hilton Hotel. I was approached to become head of a company producing a series of films for television celebrating the early days of the industry. It became apparent that the company would be only producing the programmes, not owning them. So it was goodbye, Bob.

Colin Sherbourne had a production company and an Australian partner, Wally Heefy. This was a slightly more attractive proposition, and although I did not take on the company's debts, I did offer Colin a contract and he directed several commercials for me.

I produced a couple of commercials for Holts, the car accessory company. The first was selling one of their DIY repair products and featured a well-known actor who was seen under a car fixing a leak in the exhaust. He had dialogue and was supposed to say "Holts have a thing for it." The first take on the rushes went well until he caught his hand on something and came out with the perfectly delivered, "Holts have a thing for it, SHIT."

The second commercial was to promote that the company charged less than its competitiors. A car was to be seen being crushed by a repair bill. To achieve this in the days before it could be created by electronic wizardry meant using a real car and a huge block of concrete with our giant bill fixed to the front. The concrete block would have to be lifted by crane and then lowered onto the car, gradually crushing it. So where to shoot it? I decided upon one of the airship hangars at RAF Cardington. All went well and we narrowly avoided disaster when the weight of crane and concrete proved too much for the hangar floor and broke through very nearly crashing onto the car and destroying the commercial.

We were asked to produce a series of three commercials for Black and Decker, the tool company, who, at the time, were riding high on the boom of the DIY industry. Over three days, we filmed tool demonstrations on various building sites and delivered three commercials. The next year we were again approached and made three further commercials.

We were asked again for the third year to work for the company, and when I looked at the script I saw that it was based on situations on a normal housing build, I realised that if I brought a builder into a studio, we could construct every sequence called for without the cost and inconvenience of travelling to locations. That year we were able to deliver four commercials for less than three had cost the previous year. There was a slight downside to this success as the client changed agencies the following year. We were again asked to produce a commercial on a totally different theme. The agency, however, did not seem very happy and were clearly of the opinion that I was too close to their client. So after four years, the relationship came to an end.

My office was always open for any client to drop in for a drink (and sometimes many more than one). On one particular evening my P.A. Jo's husband, who was a producer at J. Walter Thompson, came into the office and said he had a test commercial that the agency had put together and could he show it to us. The idea was incredibly simple and featured a close-up of an eye with a soundtrack telling a story as the eye from time to time blinked to the sound of a camera shutter. The commercial was for Kodak. It was a brilliant idea and my reaction was immediate, I wanted to produce the final commercial. In fact, we made two or three commercials, but shooting them was not nearly as simple as the idea.

The actor or actress for the eye needed to have their head held in a rigid position and then blink to order, but that did not provide the final image that was wanted for the commercial. In those days, there were no video facilities companies that could create the requisite images. So when, as on one commercial, we needed a tear to well up in the eye to note the birth of a baby, there was nothing for it but to create the effect frame by frame. It was very time-consuming and required a degree of skill on the part of the editor. I spent one whole evening editing that particular commercial myself just because I was so demanding, and had considerably more patience than my director.

We were subsequently asked to produce another commercial based on a children's birthday party, and we needed a garden location. We used a house belonging to one of the agency executives. It was a tall Georgian house in Greenwich and I was particularly impressed with the array of family portraits hanging on the staircase, each oil painting clearly labelled with the name of a particular ancestor. I commented on the impressive display and was told that they were all paintings picked up in sales and bore no relationship whatsoever to the family. It just goes to show how easily we are all taken in.

I was asked to produce a shampoo commercial for a small agency, Pembertons. The commercial was shot in Venice. Needless to say, this provided the usual problems associated with filming in Italy. The agency had in their wisdom cast a pop singer, Peter Noone of Herman's Hermits, and at the end of the commercial he was called upon to embrace the female featured in the spot. Unfortunately, there was a problem as he was married and his wife objected to the proposed action. I don't recall how the conflict was resolved, but she evidently did not trust her husband.

We had to shoot a pack shot in London to appear as though it was shot in Venice. A tall order you might think, but actually quite simple. We took over a small studio in Soho and made a shallow tray lined with black plastic. I paid a workman who was repairing pavements in Mayfair half a crown for a paving stone and set it up in front of the tray now filled with water as though it was a parapet of a bridge.

With several pencils suitably coloured to look like the Venetian posts in the canal, the effect was indistinguishable from a real location as the focus was on the product and the background was a soft focus impression.

Despite not being a member of the union, I was running a successful production company and, of course, had dealings with the union from time to time. One director in particular who worked for me as a freelance was very left-wing and if he was working we could be sure of a visit from a union organiser and a possible ticket inspection. The union in the sixties seemed to be intent on sending delegations to Moscow or Havana, and it was not to buy cigars! On one day I was shooting a Dulux commercial at my own home in Chislehurst and had another shoot going on at a studio in Greenwich that was visited by a union rep.

The studio shoot was under-crewed by one man and there was trouble.

The producer in charge rang me at home and I had to sort out the situation. What the union did not know – and I was not about to tell them – was that I was sitting on the stairs in my own home where I was shooting with an American cameraman and one assistant breaking every rule in the book. Some years later I was having lunch with one of the rather more approachable union reps who I got on quite well with when I happened to say, "One day, you'll let me into the union." He looked at me in surprise and said, "You're a member, aren't you?" "No," came my reply, "you have never let me in."

The following week I had a union ticket that allowed me to produce or direct in film or television. I never paid any subs and neither, I suspect, did many others, or if they did they would pay at the rate applicable to a much lower grade. Many years later on my return from location in Antigua, I was paged at Heathrow and told by the deputy chairman of the company I was then working for that, if asked, I was to say that I had been on a particular shoot where the company had been caught out. I was pretty cross as the company had paid up my dues just to keep themselves out of trouble. Not all technicians were keen union members and those that were may well have been the losers as one would not willingly book a troublemaker.

Directors could sometimes be a problem for different reasons and I recall two particular instances when I felt that Cliff Owen was being especially bloody-minded. The first instance was on a shoot for Kellogg's Cornflakes and featured a man who had just moved house and could not find his cereal bowl for breakfast. The result was a large helping in a mixing bowl. It was the last set up before lunch and the actor had to start eating from the unusually large bowl. Cliff kept going take after take and completed some thirty before calling an end to the man's torture.

Two or three years later, Cliff was to do the same again on the last take before lunch, but this time it was a young man supposedly having his first taste of Guinness.

There was no excuse for treating actors in this way and it was never the last take that was the best. Years later, I had a more serious falling out with Cliff, but that is still to come.

Other directors were not a problem, and one in particular was the only person who put commercials for the company on equal terms with his feature commitments. His name was Ted Kotcheff, and to work with him was a real pleasure. On one occasion he came to a pre-production meeting with the agency in my office and when leaving asked if the date was now fixed. I confirmed that it was and he said that he was due for a costume fitting on his next feature on that day, but he would change it. Other directors would run a mile at the first whiff of a feature.

The annual Advertising Film Festival, originally held alternatively in Venice or Cannes, but latterly only in Cannes, became almost an annual event, and looking back the overall impression certainly in the early days was that there were an awful lot of young people spending other people's money and pretending that it was normal. In later years, it became rather more serious and there was less bad behaviour. My wife and I were to attend festivals in Venice on at least three occasions and some six in Cannes. We stayed in four different hotels in Cannes, one in La Napoule and one in Roquefort-les-Pins, a truly lovely hotel I had discovered when on a recce for a Coca-Cola location.

Only one or two memories are worth mentioning, one when with the family in our Volvo estate, we had an oil seal go en route and ended up arriving in Cannes on the back of a truck. I was very relieved to find that our hotel – which that year was not on the front – was practically next door to the local Volvo dealer.

On another occasion we decided to give a DIY party organised by my director, Frank Worth, his wife and Shirley and myself. The idea was simple, informal and a lot more fun than many of the rather boring cocktail parties. We hired a boat usually used for ferrying people to the offshore islands, bought two children's paddling pools and placing one on either side of the boat filled them with ice from the local ice factory and dozens of bottles of champagne bought on sale or return. Soft drinks and snacks were a simple case of visiting the supermarket. We set off into the bay to visit an island and the whole thing was a huge success primarily because it was so relaxed and informal. I was told that next day the bay was full of floating champagne bottles, but I rather doubt it. Each year at the end of the festival there was a last night dinner, a buffet, and over the years, we would joke that the Germans would sharpen their elbows in order to get at the food first. It was only a slight exaggeration but those of us in the know started to arrange our own last night dinners to avoid the crush.

One year in particular I booked a table at a favourite restaurant in one of the hilltop villages and took the trouble to visit it to select the wines. During the day I met a client and asked if he would like to join our party. He politely declined saying that he had his own client to look after. I said I had two spare seats and told him his client would be more than welcome, so he finally accepted. The wines I had selected were a Meursault to start, Claret with the main course and a dessert wine. I was completely unaware that my agency friend's client was a major wine company and two of the three wines I had chosen were their very best. Phew!

Neither the client nor the agency would ever believe that I had not arranged it.

There is a lot of food advertising on television and a lot of waste. Of course one has to be very careful of anything left out under lights and this was particularly the case when I made a commercial for Fray Bentos featuring a fully-stocked butchers shop and the wonderful Bernard Cribbins as our butcher. We had a professional butcher with us who made the decisions as to what could be kept and what should be discarded. All left over food that was still useable was always sent on to a charity for the homeless in west London, but there were times when this was not possible.

If you were advertising a brand new product, it could well be top secret and any leftover packages had to be sealed in black sacks and disposed of. There were, and probably still are, one or two small tricks that can be employed to give a slightly better look to the product than might otherwise be the case. Slightly smaller plates and knives and forks can make a portion appear larger. "Every little helps," says the Tesco slogan and they were for some time certainly a help to my company. I first worked in a Tesco in Wimbledon on a Fairy liquid commercial with Simon Dee, the disc jockey. The store had a car park on the roof and a manager I got on well with. The Fairy shoot was followed by a spot for Cadbury Fruit & Nut and then a commercial for Danish Bacon. I remember the date of the bacon shoot. It was the day my son was born and there were complications, so I was not on the location.

When Michael Frewin was with me we had several contracts with the Irish. They were mainly domestic products, but finally we landed one for Aer Lingus, the national airline. How they came to employ a small English company to make a commercial for *their* national airline heaven only knows, but there we were at Shannon Airport looking at their newly arrived Jumbo jet. It was the first time I had seen, let alone been aboard, one and to see it on the tarmac alongside a BAC One Eleven really did emphasise just how big it was. The plane still had its Boeing training crew who were there to train the Irish pilots. The chief pilot of Aer Lingus was a Captain Little. We filmed inside and outside the aircraft and out on the tarmac as Captain Little carried out a series of circuits and landings for our benefit. My camera crew out near the runway did what crews are liable to do and pushed their luck to get closer to the landing plane. They were probably unaware of the fact that the plane's wings were wider than the runway and, as a result, when the engines were boosted for take off after just touching down, the crew, camera and tripod were all blown over. What did not blow over, however, was the argument in the Irish parliament over the choice of our company that got them into quite a stew.

When I was asked to make a commercial for another Heinz brand featuring a group of cub scouts out camping, the original thought was to cast the cubs from theatre schools and then wardrobe them. I was a father with children at a small private school that actually had a cub pack. So as a member of the Parent Teacher Association, why not kill two birds with one stone? It was relatively simple to arrange with all those taking part having permission from their parents and a payment made to the school. The school was in West Wickham and we were soon setting up camp on Hayes Common. A very enthusiastic band of cubs was soon singing and queuing up for the delights of Heinz beans and bacon burgers, kept in line by their cub mistress, Damaris Hayman. It was a genuine win-win situation and the boys were all superb. I used the school again for a Fairy toilet soap commercial in which my younger daughter played a key role. It was just common sense.

Michael Frewin was costing the company too much and not attracting the work that he claimed he had lost because he had joined me. That claim made little sense as we were profitable and his previous employer had gone bust.

Michael asked that his retainer be paid into an account in the Cayman Islands and was becoming a liability, so he had to go and again I changed the name of the company, this time to Geoffrey Forster Associates, which is probably what it should have been from the start.

I have already mentioned some of the approaches I had received from other companies in varying degrees of difficulty, but there were two that were on a different and much more acceptable basis. They came from two different producer and director pairs. One was from a producer who had worked for me in the company, but without much success. He had now teamed up with a director and wanted to start a new company. The second approach came from an ex-client of mine who had been a producer at Young & Rubicam, and had teamed up with another producer turned director. We had enough space in Curzon Street to enable me to offer each pair office space with very little alteration and I formed a new company called Group 31 to provide services to each of the pairs and my own company. Two new companies were formed, Morgan and Mount, who occupied the front office, previously reception and a new partition wall being built to create a passage through to the large central office, and Radio Pictures, which had the room at the rear of the basement opening into Market Mews.

The principle was very simple, the business had moved on and any production was in effect self-financing, all the companies needed was an office. I drew up a contract that enabled each company to operate on a very limited rental to cover all the shared services – reception, accounts, telephone and telex.

There was then a charge for other services that were only used when working on a production, such as the editing department. The scheme depended upon a strictly first come, first served basis, which had to include my own company and it worked very well. There were safeguards to ensure a minimum contribution from each company and there was to be a profit share at the end of the year based on contributions. The benefit to Geoffrey Forster Associates was an immediate saving of £22,000 a year on the cost of our overheads. Morgan and Mount became very successful, Radio Pictures less so and the scheme ran until at the rent review after seven and a half years, I decided to move from Curzon Street and relocate in Soho.

Over the years my advice has been sought by agencies about possible new employees. I was not the only one, I knew of two others whose advice was sought. One person who usually talked to me was Gilbert King, the television head of Young & Rubicam which was a major client of mine with brands like Heinz, Flash, Fairy liquid and Zerox among others, including the aforementioned British Rail. They represented nearly 40% of our turnover. I had been on holiday and on my first day back at work I found myself in Gilbert's office. He asked me about a particular producer that I just happened to have worked with fairly recently. I knew that he was not a suitable employee for the agency and said so. There was a silence, after which Gilbert said, "That's a pity. I have just taken him on."

It was probably two or three months later that I took Gilbert to lunch at the White House restaurant. It was the 6 February, 1970, and I have good cause to remember the date. Over lunch I was told that he had a recording of the producer in question asking a production company for cash for placing a contract. I was shocked and surprised and not entirely sure that such a story could be true.

If it was, then presumably the recording must have come from the company concerned and could be produced. I knew that if I had been proved correct, Gilbert would have lost face and that would have been something he could not envisage. Was there, I thought, an element of self-justification in what I was being told? I was working with one of his producers on a new contract for Fairy liquid featuring Barbara Murray, and I repeated the story to him.

An internal investigation took place in the agency and eventually reached the time when I had a call from my contact to say that the matter could not be taken further unless I was prepared to repeat the story in front of Gilbert. It so happened that on the very evening of that call, Shirley and I were going with my contact producer to the Rothman's tennis final at the Royal Albert Hall, so I agreed to go to the agency en route. I sat in Gilbert's office and told him when we had had lunch and of the conversation. As a result, the producer was paid off and I made a lot of friends, but lost a lot of business. But not P&G business. That would have been too difficult for Gilbert to withhold.

I have previously mentioned the director, Ted Kotcheff. He certainly became a very reliable member of our team always putting his work for the company on an equal footing with his work on features. I recall particularly a Fairy liquid commercial with Tony Blackburn. We had set up on location a village fete and Tony was in charge of a hoopla stall. The location was almost certainly what has now become Thorpe Park. Ted was abroad when we set up and was only due back the day before the shoot. I sent a car to the airport for him and he arrived on the location with a fully prepared shooting script. I know of no other director of his standing who would have done that!

Ted was spending more and more time in his native Canada, but came back to the UK from time to time and combined commercial shoots with visits to his family in London, but he was planning to remain on the other side of the Atlantic and I knew that I could not keep him here forever. The last job Ted directed for me was for Xerox and it was for Young & Rubicam, despite the previous confrontation with Gilbert King. I did still have one firm friend in the agency, Graham Terry, who was also a big fan of Ted. The commercial meant building a replica of the Globe Theatre and we did this in Elstree Studios. Ironically, there was already a replica set across the road in the television studio, but we could not make use of it. The story of the commercial was that a rehearsal was in progress but the final text had not been completed and copies were needed ASAP. Enter a scribe with photocopies, courtesy of Xerox, which duly saved the day.

I had not expected any further approaches or offers of money, but I was wrong. One came from a very unexpected source. Namely, Gilbert King, who had clearly buried the hatchet and wanted to talk to me about taking over the company, Anglo Scottish. They were the owners of Halliford Studios and seemed successful and stable. They also had another large share of Procter & Gamble business, so that may have been an influencing factor. It was suggested that I should go and talk to them about a link. I went to have lunch with the board and it went very well until one of the older members said, "We should never have let agencies tell us how to make commercials." The board was clearly living in the past and was obviously completely out of touch with the times, so that was that.

There was one more approach and it really would have been a coup, but circumstances would dictate otherwise. Pearl & Dean, who were still represented on my board, did a reverse takeover of British Lion, which included Shepperton Studios.

I was asked to look at the studio and particularly their sponsored film activities comprising Lion Television, a relatively new video company, and Littleton Park Productions, a documentary company. I visited the studio and had a meeting with Andy Worker, the current studio manager. I came away with full details of the documentary company and a feeling that the studio was living in the past.

I put together my report that took into account the existing overseas production units of P&D and my own company, and the facilities of British Lion. There were great possibilities and my proposals were well received. My proposal was put to the British Lion board and there followed a lunch with John Frazer of P&D (still on my board) and Roy Boulting, representing British Lion. The following day I received an offer to become managing director of the new enterprise.

My acceptance goes without saying, but in a sudden swoop, the details of which I really do not understand, a certain John Bentley came on the scene. I submitted a copy of my report to his assistant, Bev Ripley, but they were asset strippers and were only interested in what they could take out of Shepperton and how much of the studio lot they could sell off for building, so the deal collapsed.

I was becoming aware that I was sending producers abroad who were not making the profit they should have been, and that my always staying in the office to look after other clients was not what I should be doing. I had sent others on my behalf to the Caribbean, to South Africa, the USA, North Africa and Europe, and it was high time for me to take back the reins.

One morning I took a call from the Procter & Gamble head office in Newcastle. It was from the head of the TV advertising department – none other than the man I took to see Stonehenge – and he wanted to know if I would take on an American production for Camay soap, which they hoped to shoot in London.

Apparently the American company had been in touch with Samuelsons, the equipment supply company, but Newcastle had recommended my company. The reason for wanting to shoot in London was that they were featuring a lady who called herself Princess Pignatelli and she did not want to work in the United States for tax reasons. She was no longer a princess, I believe, and had remarried the American photographer, Richard Avedon. Be that as it may, I agreed to service the Yanks. We needed a large stage for two sets and by chance Bray

Studios on the Thames had just been reopened as Bray International, and they were available.

The American company arrived in my office in the shape of not one but two directors, one nominally in charge, the second a dialogue director, David Negata. They also brought with them their own cameraman, but I of course had to pay lip service to the union. I booked an English cameraman and told him to remain on call until midday each day after which he was free. The sets were classic Georgian in style, a bedroom with a dressing table with three mirrors and a sitting room.

There were no problems to speak of on the shoot, but I certainly had one or two when I saw rushes. The American cameraman, who was his own operator, managed to photograph the crew tracking across the shot in the dressing table mirror! When it came to the sitting room, there was a large marble fireplace which displayed a gaping black hole which any English operator would have either avoided altogether or filled with a display of flowers. I was seeing a set of rushes that I would never have accepted from an English crew, and it was a classic example of what I already knew, that we had in the UK the best technicians in the world. The Americans went off satisfied and we were paid service fees that made the job well worth taking on.

It may be appropriate at this point to look back at the history of the company. When we started, I had given Norman Burrows a 20% shareholding, and as already stated, I had to fire him after the first year. Not very easy as his solicitor attended each AGM held at our accountants in the city – or tried to, at least. They were always late, so we simply closed the meetings before they arrived. Michael Frewin was another mistake, and I had to cancel his contract before his demands put the company in jeopardy. In fact, as Michael had already caused problems with a mounting list of creditors, I took drastic action. I arranged a meeting with Les Osliffe, the head of Rank Laboratories in Denham, and the financial director. I told them that we had a cash flow problem and as they were my biggest creditor, I proposed to pay off all other creditors whilst putting their amount on hold, saying that I was confident of sorting out the problem and that they would eventually be paid in full. It was to be one of the best business decisions I ever made. They told me that they had several other companies paying off debts and we became very good friends from then on.

I kept to my side of the bargain and by being honest and up front enhanced my standing in the business yet again. Having had to argue my case with the board of P&D for even minor changes, one of the first things I noticed was that I had no one to argue with. It was quite a lonely feeling, every decision was mine and I "carried the can".

When you are the boss of a company based entirely on your own ability, you become very aware of the responsibility and may make decisions based on your commitments rather than for creative reasons that could have given the company a higher profile. I remember thinking that I had five wives and twelve children whose livelihoods depended on my ability to bring in the work.

Shirley's mother was an invalid, having suffered a stroke when Shirley was just three years old. It was at about this time that her father suffered a heart attack and despite recovering to the extent that we were able to transfer him to a nursing home near Guilford, an area he had known in his youth, he died and we became responsible for looking after Shirley's mother and finding a suitable home where she could be looked after at weekends. To cut a long story short, that is what prompted our move to Sussex, where we were able to buy a large house with wheelchair access. Our previous town house in Chislehurst – where I had shot the Dulux commercial that the client eventually decided was too up market for them – just wasn't unsuitable.

The company had established several very strong relationships with clients and agencies, several of which were to last for many years. I had an excellent staff and it is interesting to note that I have always had very good and loyal employees, but disastrous partners, with the obvious exception of Robert Amram, who was going from strength to strength. He had been directing documentaries in Mexico with a local producer as partner and had won an Oscar for one of his productions.

I hope my readers will bear with me if I now include something I wrote forty years ago and found again only recently when turning out some old files. It illustrates clearly my state of mind at the time and that I was looking for a new challenge.

I wrote the following in June 1973, as I travelled up to London from Buxted Station in Sussex. It was a time when I was starting to realise that running my own company had become a problem as I would never be able to sell a company so dependent on just one individual. I had been sending other producers abroad with mixed results. While I felt I had to remain in London to run the business and service our major clients, I was, in many ways, too comfortable and becoming lazy. I needed a new challenge. Perhaps to get out and produce? Later the same year, I was to find it.

"Good morning," said the young man as he came to a halt at the usual point on the platform. "Good morning," came the reply and then unexpectedly, "Looks as though summer's here at last." "I certainly hope so, it's about time," replied G, closing the conversation and wondering if any other words would pass between them before tomorrow's salutation.

He stood looking out across the Sussex countryside basking in the strong early morning sun whilst his companion, dark suited and bowler hatted returned to his copy of The Times. G was in his late thirties, blond, five feet eleven inches, slim with blue eyes and that fine hair that blows all over the place in the slightest breath of air. Having only recently had it cut, it was at the moment reposing fairly neatly over his ears and around the top of his collar. It still was fairly obvious from the length of his hair and the silver identity bracelet and ring on his right hand that he was not one of the usual group of city directors and businessmen who had formed the regular band of first class passengers from this tiny Sussex station for the past few years.

True, he made his gesture to conformity as he stood there, a copy of The Times under his right arm that reached down to the handle of a battered black briefcase. He wore black trousers with a navy casual jacket over a white shirt and black tie. A year earlier he would have gone to the office on such a morning wearing only a floral shirt, jeans and a pair of casual shoes, but then he had been living nearer London and travelling to the office every day in his sports car.

It was two months since he and his family had moved to the small village of Buxted, nestling among the farms of East Sussex not far from the Ashdown Forest. And it was two months that had had a most disturbing influence on him.

The diesel train chugged around the bend and approached the station; signs of life from the thirty or so waiting passengers as they anticipated just where their compartment would stop. G climbed into a First Class non-smoker and settled in his usual corner facing the engine on the left. The two passengers sat in their opposite corners, bowler hat reading The Times, G clutching his copy on his lap staring vacantly out of the window. He enjoyed the journey. it was strangely relaxing to travel through such beautiful countryside twice a day. Ashdown Forest, the farms, the oast houses, he wondered what the journey would be like in winter; but to hell with that, there was a whole summer to come yet!

G often enjoyed looking at property from the train, the only trouble was that however idyllic the setting when viewed from the comfort of the 8.30, one had to remember that breakfast on that sunlit terrace meant in fact breakfast overlooking the main line to London. The train pulled out of another station and as it did a farm came into view, a white weatherboarded house under a weathered tile roof. The main house dressed in creeper and guarded by rhododendrons in full display. To the right, set slightly behind, was a yard with an immaculately kept barn leading to an oast, whilst behind the house and away to the left stretched hop fields with their myriad strings waiting to be climbed. In front of the property, a well trimmed lawn ran some fifty or sixty feet down to a road separated from the railway by a field in which six cows grazed lazily. The train gathered speed and a cock pheasant watched as the wheels clattered by above his head.

The move to the country, something that G and his wife had talked about on many occasions, had finally been both prompted and made possible by the death of his father- in-law, not that he or his wife had come into any money but responsibility for an invalid mother-in-law had enabled them to borrow some capital short-term to finance the move to a larger house and he had been determined that such a move would be to the country. In the last few weeks, he had been working furiously on the house. There was much work to be done and no money to bring in expensive contractors, quite apart from the fact that G had an inborn distrust of builders and would infinitely prefer to carry out the work himself, which he did to a very high standard.

Apart from the odd day he had taken off here and there, he found himself in the same seat on the 8.30 every morning. The train pulled into another station and with a series of shuddering jerks the passengers knew that they were now attached to the four coaches that had awaited their arrival. G found it hard to explain exactly what was bothering him, he found himself surveying his companions, solid pillars of business in city uniforms, his education had given him the ability to feel perfectly at ease with them. His own sober if casual dress was a conscious attempt on his part to ensure that they would feel comfortable in his presence. This consciousness of other people's feelings and an almost chameleon-like quality of being able to adapt himself to any level of society had been, he considered, one of his most important attributes, it had certainly stood him in good stead as a manager and negotiator at various times in the past.

Somehow G had never been able to explain this feeling for people to his wife, who accused him on many occasions of changing his mind or reproached him for his speech when talking to some less well-educated group of people. She found it impossible to accept that he felt completely at ease with people in any environment and, quite naturally, fell in with the surrounding style and conversation. There was something undeniably solid about his traveling companions, and to his annoyance, he found himself envying their respectable upper middle class lives with their obvious security. Security was perhaps the key to his present feeling of unrest, he had known little of it as a child and virtually none in his business life, through choice in this case. Now, for the first time as he approached forty, he found himself envying men who had the security of birth, upbringing and a certain wealth, men who certainly had no worries as to where the next mortgage payment was coming from and whether or not they could afford a holiday this year. It was, he mused, not so much a question of security, he still cared little for that, rather one of increasing frustration.

To be sure, he could live in a smaller house and submerge himself in the quicksands of suburbia, but that he knew would be the end of all interest in home and would, he suspected, lead him to walk out on everything in the end. His philosophy over the past twenty odd years had been simple. If more money was needed, it was up to him to earn it and he had been fortunate enough to be able to live by this philosophy until now. He had enjoyed his working life to date, but now felt an overwhelming desire to change it.

The trouble was that circumstances had forced him into a job that he had not chosen and despite having succeeded to the point where he was his own master and had been for many years he now found himself dissatisfied with the work he was doing. He was increasingly frustrated by the lack of control he could exercise over his own future, and the lack of integrity that he still found amongst the people he was called upon to work with. He longed to be able to tell some of his clients exactly what he thought of them and their attitudes. In short, he yearned to be allowed to do a good job, something he knew he was more than capable of doing. He had never yet failed at anything he had attempted to do and was intensely aware that his best work was always done when under pressure of one kind or another. Part of the trouble was that he was involved in the business of selling and he was not, and never would be, a salesman. He was a good executive and organizer, but had made two bad mistakes when choosing partners.

The train pulled into a station, they were nearing London now and the proportion of semi-detached houses was growing mile by mile as they sprawled into the fields and woods. G uncrossed his legs and drew in his feet as an elderly man got in, small, perhaps nearing seventy but still with a good head of silver hair topped by a curiously boater-like felt hat that G could not put a name to. He was a regular traveller. G had seen him many times before and wondered what could possibly take him to London so often. Always smartly dressed in a light grey suit and wearing a bow tie. He had a bright eye, alert and oddly contrasting with the fact that his body appeared to be in imminent danger of shrinking to the point where his hands and feet no longer protruded from his suit.

G had been distracted from his brooding, he came back to reality and told himself that it was all nonsense. He couldn't really blame others, or circumstances, when the remedy was in his own hands. He could make the effort if only he knew which way to push, that was the real crunch, he simply did not know what he wanted to do. The clouds of depression gathered again as the first concrete office blocks came into view and G began

to think back, to try to find some clue to where he had
taken the wrong road.

It was not, of course, true to say that I had taken the
wrong road, I had clearly made the right career moves
at each stage so far but the business had grown up and
I felt the need to get back to being a hands-on producer.
I needed a new challenge and there was only one place
that I was likely to find it, James Garrett and Partners,
the one company I had always regarded as a challenge
when we were in competition.

8

PRODUCING RESULTS

Garretts was, if not the only other company controlled by a producer, then certainly the largest and most successful. I would not only enjoy the challenge of producing, but knew that I would find the company itself a challenge. I had made my decision and rang up Jim and arranged a meeting, suggesting that he needed a good producer! A deal was agreed and I started to close my business down. I gave his company car to my editor and settled all outstanding bills. We never had a debt and closed with no creditors. I retained the company, Group 31, and was paid through it by Garretts for the first year. I remember very little of the closing details, but changed employer within a day or two.

A great friend of mine, Mike Gilmour, had been taken into my confidence and we agreed that once I had made the change, we would have lunch to celebrate. At Garretts, there were two producers in each office and I found myself sharing space and a secretary with the producer who had insisted on my going to dinner so that he could suggest himself as my managing director. His name was John Byrne. Only then did it dawn on me that he must have been offered a job there and must have been under pressure to give an answer, hence the urgency to approach me.

After a day or two, Mike and I had our lunch at the White Elephant Club, three or four doors down from my old address in Curzon Street. On my return to the office, John told me that I was treading on peoples toes, or words to that effect, and that Mike was his client. Not any more I am afraid, our relationship was far too strong and would in years to come prove both a great advantage to the company and a huge source of irritation to Jim.

When I joined, the company had a budgeting office; producers were not responsible for their own production budgets. This system was anathema to me and very soon I became the only producer allowed to prepare budgets for their own productions. After all, I had designed my own very comprehensive form which, along with that from another senior producer, became the industry standard. I was also particularly unimpressed with the production office, again run by someone without my experience and knowledge.

One of my first jobs was to film a commercial for The American League of Women Voters. It was a charity appeal made by Cary Grant and I directed it on the original *Great Gatsby* set at Pinewood Studios. I was appalled by the quality of the sound recorded by the crew booked by the production office, and made sure that on my next production, I used the team that I had used for several years previously. From then on they became the regular sound crew for the company!

The company had been, and continued to be, very successful, but had a bad reputation for additional charges after the contract had been signed and for switch selling when a director became unavailable, hardly surprising when the producers were given so little responsibility. In short, the company was run on too rigid lines that were dictated by Jim Garrett himself, and he would brook no argument. I was at one time promised the managing directorship of the company, but this failed to materialise.

My relationship with Procter & Gamble continued to the benefit of the company and we became one of their major suppliers. I even had star director, Nic Roeg, the director of *Walkabout, Don't Look Now, The Man Who Fell To Earth* and other features working on their business, much to everyone's amazement.

After my Cary Grant commercial, I was to be involved in another Triumph spot. The commercial had already been cast and was to be directed by Dick Clement, who later in partnership with Ian La Frenais, was to gain fame as the writer of many television sitcoms including *Auf Wiedersehen Pet* and *Porridge*. The location was in Bromley Kent, an area I knew well. The commercial opened in a bedroom where a young man was very nearly caught in bed by a returning husband. The young man exits through a window onto a flat garage roof, clad only in a towel and makes his getaway. We see him enter a car showroom of Triumph cars. He approaches the rather superior assistant and demands, "a test drive in a very fast car."

The assistant was played by Frank Thornton, alias Captain Peacock of *Are You Being Served*, who also just happened to be a cousin of my mother. We see them driving as the assistant details the car's features when suddenly another car pulls alongside driven by the irate husband shaking his fist. Our salesman and hero turn into a parking area and our hero jumps out to make his getaway still clad only in his towel.

As he sprints up a grassy hillside making for a distant wood, his towel drops away and we are left with a distant image of the naked man running away from the camera.

The rules governing the use of children in commercials are very strict and dictate the amount of time a child can spend on set according to age, as well as many other conditions. In the early days, the conditions were often ignored and children could well find themselves putting in hours well in excess of the rules. I remember one commercial when we were filming a children's game in a playroom and my director, Richard Loncraine, was for some long forgotten reason, running very late indeed. In those circumstances it fell to me to keep the mothers happy and ensure completion of the day's schedule.

The lady of the house made us sandwiches and tea and eventually we completed the shoot. Many years later, when my wife and I had moved to the village of Lindfield in Sussex, we were invited to a New Year's party at a rather grand house in the village. Soon after we arrived, I was approached by a lady who produced a photograph of me as a cameraman at someone's wedding where she and her husband had been guests. It seems we had mutual friends, and even more surprising was the fact that it had been their house near Kingston where I had filmed in their playroom some six or seven years previously.

I was asked to produce a commercial for Datsun cars, the Bluebird and Sunny, and this was to become the start of a relationship with the client and his small agency in Chelsea that was to last for several years. It also gave rise to the situation where I had to tell the cameraman that I would no longer work with his operator when I saw a reflection of the camera in the side of the car in rushes.

I mentioned the rules covering the use of children in commercials, but as a producer and father, I had other concerns for the welfare of the many children and babies I was to work with over the years. One of the very earliest commercials I made with Kenneth Hume was shot on location in rather cold conditions. It featured a three- or four-year-old, and I was very aware of the child getting cold. Years later when I had become a consultant, I was asked by Procter & Gamble to produce a Pampers commercial featuring a young child feeding ducks in the local park. It was not the right time of year and I immediately decided that we would build the duck pond in a studio. I rang an art director I knew could handle the job and, to cut a long story short, the set was so convincing and so well lit by my chosen cameraman that the senior management at P&G would not believe it had been a studio shoot.

At the other end of the scale I had a shoot with a baby for Johnson's baby oil in a studio when the cameraman used so much light so close to the child's head that I very nearly had to stop the shoot. That particular problem arose because the director's choice of cameraman was one who always used very high light levels and had a reputation based on a stylish showreel, not his suitability for our particular job.

The commercial was very simple and involved a young mum with her baby lying on their fronts head-to-head on a white towelling background. They were both naked as the camera tracked slowly along the body of the young lady coming to rest on the baby. The voice-over spoke gently of the benefits of the product and as nothing, even the hint of a breast was shown, it was gentle and could not have offended anyone. The problem for the producers, from the agency and the production company, was that the artist had to have perfect skin with no birthmarks or suntan marks. An afternoon had to be spent shut in a small casting studio looking at naked girls. It was tough but someone had to do it!

Despite my continuing relationship with Procter & Gamble, I was soon asked to produce a Persil commercial for their major competitor Unilever. The idea was simple, two boys, one using a garden hose to wash mud from his bicycle. The obvious happens and he sprays mud all over his companion's tee shirt. My mother-in-law had recently died, and with the small inheritance my wife received, we decided to have a swimming pool put in our garden. The excavation resulted in a large amount of mud in the garden so I volunteered to bring a bucket of mud to the location. The shoot went very well on day one and the tee shirt was taken away by the client to be washed overnight. DISASTER! The next morning the client turned up to say that they had been unable to remove the stain. Apparently my particular mud had some sort of ochre content that made the stain indelible.

The Bluebell Railway in Sussex was always popular with the grandchildren especially when they ran the Santa Express or the Thomas the Tank Engine trains, but it was also a very frequently used location, and as I lived close by, very convenient. The first time I shot there was for a supermarket that has long since disappeared, Keymarkets. The script was written like a silent film and we cast a group of character actors to play the Keymarket Cops. We had, of course, the obligatory maiden tied to the tracks as the train approached and her predictable rescue by the Keymarket Cops. The cast was all wardrobed as old-time police and a key part of the uniform was white gloves. Unfortunately, the wardrobe mistress had left the gloves behind so I sent one of our regular drivers off to the local town to buy some. The camera set up was a good quarter of a mile from our base at a bridge from where we could climb up to the track. We were set up without the gloves when the driver was seen running along the track towards us. Thinking the gloves were coming, we waited for him to arrive. When he did so it was to show me a sample for approval as he thought they were rather expensive. To send him back would have cost us at least another hour and our heroine would have long since died under the wheels of the train!

I would not give that driver such an important task again.

Some time later I was to work with the Bluebell Railway again, but in rather different circumstances. I was to produce a commercial for Cadbury and the bookstall on the platform had to be converted to a sweet stall with all Cadbury brands on display. The director was, Michael Lindsay-Hogg, whom I was to work with on several occasions.

The star of the commercial was Cilla Black, and I had arranged accommodation for her and Bobby, her husband, at a local hotel that had a good reputation and where I knew the restaurant was top rate. My wife and I arranged a dinner for Cilla and Bobby and naturally asked Michael to join us. He declined the invitation which I felt was rather bad manners but I put it down to shyness. My wife and I enjoyed a very pleasant dinner with Cilla and Bobby on a day, as it turned out, was their wedding anniversary. What happened to all that chocolate you may well ask? The location was very near the Chailey Heritage Hospital and school for disabled children and it became the recipient of a carload of chocolate bars of all shapes and sizes.

When we had moved into our house in the village of Buxted, the railway line from the local station was due to be electrified in 1976. Here we are forty-two years later and counting – and the local population is still waiting!

One day I was approached to make a commercial for the car component company, Lucas. The storyboard showed a formation of cars forming the name Lucas in a large clear space. Many of the cars would be in position and only the last six or seven out of a total of something like seventy or eighty would be seen driving into their allotted places. We found the perfect location on the huge barrack square in Aldershot and were able to get permission to film there. We had to build a scaffolding tower for the camera and another to house two kilowatt signalling lights to cue the drivers. Today, of course, it would be a simple video compilation, but we had to shoot for real. All went well with not a major problem but the client wanted two versions, one in daylight and one at night. Having effectively shot the daytime version, it was a simple matter of repeating it at night. Or was it? Only the cars actually driving had drivers who could keep the headlights on and the batteries of the static cars would not last out so the cars had to be fitted with small generators to overcome the problem. That done we were able to carry on but it was getting late and the parade ground being near the married quarters we did get a few complaints about the noise. Next morning, we took down our scaffolding and disappeared never to darken their doorstep again! It was only later that I discovered that one of my regular travelling companions from Buxted was a director of Lucas and he confirmed that the spot had been a success and had raised their share value.

In 1974, I was asked to produce a commercial for J&B Whisky. The script had been looked at by several companies and the agency producer, Ray, had done a recce. Quite by chance I had taken with him a location manager who had previously worked as my production manager, so I knew that I could rely on his report. One thing that always has to be considered is the amount of travelling time involved in any location shoot. Film crews have to be paid for travelling time, in addition to the filming time, and this is a cost that is not reflected in the final product on screen. Just occasionally travel time can be built into the schedule and this was never truer than on this production.

The story was of a husband returning home to find that his wife had left him. Their relationship was then reprised through a series of flashbacks as she travelled across Europe through a number of familiar locations to the hotel where they first met. When she finally arrives and takes a drink on the lakeside terrace, the barman brings a bottle and glasses and, surprised, she looks up to see her husband and the inevitable reconciliation takes place. The featured flashbacks were to be at a restaurant in Paris where a trick of the light led our heroine to think back to her last meal there with her husband, seeing a view of rooftops reminding her of a postcard she was writing in a pavement cafe whilst waiting for her husband to finish a business meeting and seeing a car travelling through the Italian countryside.

The journey involved shooting in London, Paris, Lausanne, and at the Villa D'Este on Lake Como and after putting forward an initial estimate, we were awarded the job to be directed by Nic Roeg. When preparing the initial estimate, I had approached French railways to enquire about hiring a train (or part thereof) to travel from Paris to Lausanne and then on to Milan. I have to admit that I was flattered to find that of the companies originally involved in quoting the only other to have made the same enquiry was one that was managed by my ex-P.A., Jo Godman. Having agreed the director, Nic Roeg, the agency set up a further recce and took with them a 16mm camera with the intention of presenting the locations to the client and showing the cameraman the sort of problems he would encounter along the way. It was this footage that gave me enough information on which to base the final budget.

My director Nic felt he needed a ten-day schedule to complete the project, but I thought we could do better and we finally agreed on seven days, subject to a possible overrun in the event of problems. Film crews are very expensive and the client had a limited budget. My job was to make the most of it. Bearing in mind that there was to be one day of filming in London, it was clearly sensible to separate this from the continental trip, thereby limiting this to six days. By shooting from Monday to Saturday, it would be possible to have the unit home for the Sunday, which otherwise would have been very costly. Based on this schedule, the planning began in earnest. Casting was put in hand to find a couple that met the requirements of the script, the length of the schedule and its increasing proximity.

Hotels were booked and arrangements made with a restaurant in Paris and the Hertz office in Lausanne. There was one train every day from Paris to Milan via Lausanne leaving Paris at 12.30 pm and arriving in Lausanne at 4.20 pm. As the train was in a distinctive livery and only ran once each day, it was clear that we would have to leave Lausanne twenty-four hours after arriving and that would mean filming our heroine picking up a hire car from Hertz, shooting the rooftop shot from a local train and filming the postcard sequence outside the Mayor's office before boarding the train for the journey on to Milan by 4.20 pm. Quite a tall order and no time for mishaps.

At this point it is worth mentioning that the local train running from Lausanne to Neufchâtel gave the best rooftop shots but, travelled past the area rather too quickly. Nic said he would need a high-speed camera for the shot, but being aware of the budget and the amount of equipment to be loaded and unloaded at various points en route, I resisted and arranged with a very helpful Swiss Rail to run two trains on the day at a reduced speed past the appropriate spot. A high-speed camera would, of course, have produced the same effect, but cost a lot, lot more. By flying an advance party with the equipment to Paris on the Sunday evening, we were able to make the best possible use of time and the schedule was agreed as follows:

Sunday   Advance party with equipment to Paris

Monday   Unit and artistes leave for Paris on first flight
Filming at restaurant in Avenue Matignon

Tuesday   Filming at Gare de Lyon in Paris
Filming on train to Lausanne
Filming on platform in Lausanne
Filming at Hertz office in Lausanne

Wednesday   Filming on train to Neufchâtel
Filming at Mayor's office
Embark on train to Milan
Rendezvous with car at given point en route

Thursday   Filming at Villa D'Este and surrounds

Friday

Saturday   Complete filming and fly to London

Monday   Filming in London

There was to be no time for retakes or mishaps along the way.

When travelling across borders with equipment, you needed a customs document called a carnet, as I explained earlier. Your carnet would list details including registered numbers for every item and there would be enough copies for customs at each stage of the trip, hence a copy for Heathrow, another for the Paris airport, one for the customs as we left France, and another for entry into Italy and finally one for Rome airport and the last one for our arrival back at Heathrow. The system, by and large, worked well but although customs officers at airports may have been familiar with the system, the same did not necessarily apply to those operating on cross-border trains, as we were to discover.

The actress, Caroline Seymour, was the final choice for the lead, with David Baron as her husband and they were both fitted for the changes of wardrobe needed for the story. The crew was booked and the cameraman told that he could only have battery-operated hand-held lights. The equipment was sent off in advance and the unit finally assembled at Heathrow on the Monday morning for the first plane to Paris. As we met, the first potential problem presented itself. Caroline's husband, who was another well-known film director, had turned up and announced that as he had just returned from a trip abroad, and was going to accompany his wife. Having a competitor travelling with the unit did not please my director, but he promised to keep a low profile and the situation was smoothed over and off we went.

Upon arrival in Paris, the crew piled into taxis and went straight to the location where the equipment was waiting for us. All personal baggage was put in a van and went straight to the hotel. We had arranged to film at the restaurant until midday, with a possible second period from 2.30 pm to 4 pm in the afternoon. In practice, nothing runs that smoothly and despite having the first shot completed by 10.30 am, we did not finish until 7 pm. Needless to say, I needed all my charm and negotiating skills to keep things going, particularly during the evening when the restaurant became very full. Most of my time was spent asking members of the public not to look at the camera or to move to other tables. The simple expedient of feeding the crew and paying the bills for anyone we inconvenienced, kept everyone happy and we departed rather later than we had hoped but still on friendly terms with the restaurateur.

Day two arrived and we assembled to shoot scenes of our heroine boarding the train at the Gare de Lyon and then load our equipment onto the train on which we had booked a complete coach simply by paying for every seat. Conveniently, we had been able to get a coach that was half seating and half baggage van, which made things much easier. On completion of filming on the platform, I was left with some fifteen minutes to pay off the local transport we had hired. What should have been simple became a nightmare as first one then two local banks and the station office refused to accept the Thomas Cook $250 worth of travellers cheques I had been issued with by the company. Getting more and more flustered, I finally managed to assemble enough cash from the crew to pay off the drivers and boarded the train with literally seconds to spare. The company always dealt with Thomas Cook as they would allow us to pick up the cheques without the usual need to sign them before leaving!

Our coach was the first one on the train and was separated from the dining car by some nine or ten coaches which gave rise to some pretty frantic scurrying backwards and forwards as of course our first scene was a dining sequence that had to be constructed in our coach. All went well until we reached the Swiss border where the customs officer boarded the train to inspect the equipment and sign the carnet. After some complicated negotiations in French, the officer pointed out that as the French customs officer had not signed the equipment out of France, he could not admit it into Switzerland.

We were, of course, already in Switzerland, whether *he* liked it or not. The French inspector was summoned and was utterly flummoxed as he hadn't the faintest idea what to do. This resulted in a three-way argument during which my grasp of the French language was put to a more severe test. As we approached Lausanne, the Swiss inspector signed the carnet and the French inspector accompanied him from the train to telephone his boss. The train was due to stop for only three minutes, during which time we had to unload everything and set up on an adjacent platform to see Caroline standing with her Gucci luggage as the train pulled out. P-A-N-I-C S-T-A-T-I-O-N-S! (Pun intended!) Just as the train was about to leave, a local service arrived and stopped between our camera and the spot where Caroline was standing. The camera was picked up and rushed a hundred yards down the platform, and thank goodness, as our train left, Caroline was also in the right place, panic over, the shot was perfect.

Next we had to cross the road to the Hertz office and shoot a sequence of Caroline picking up a BMW, which we arranged to be brought in from Zurich. Caroline was to be seen driving through the Italian countryside in one of the flashback sequences. All very well, but we needed Caroline with the unit the next day, so the car was driven away by the agency writer and art director, complete with Caroline's hat. They had been given instructions to be at a certain point on the road over the border where the railway ran parallel with the road for several kilometres. We had calculated the time when the train would reach the spot and intended to have the camera set up in the corridor to get the flashback shot.

Our third day started with the assistant director, cameraman and one assistant taking the train to

Neufchâtel, as planned. Meanwhile, I took the rest of the unit to the next location, a pavement café, the window of which would reflect the flashback of Caroline seeing her husband. The café owner was somewhat bemused to have a film crew taking over his pavement tables but was soon pacified by the amount of coffee, red wine and omelettes being consumed. On time, we were joined by the rest of the crew, and the sequence was completed shortly before we had to be back on our train at 4.20 pm. Swiss Rail had given us complimentary seat reservations for the next part of our journey, or so we thought. In fact, when we boarded the train, we discovered that our seats were taken and had to negotiate with a very helpful American couple to vacate the seats we needed to carry on filming. There were no seats for the crew and we found ourselves camping in the corridor. The equipment we needed was piled up in every available corner and a great deal more was in the baggage van. Caroline was sitting on the floor between coaches changing clothes when the headwaiter appeared seeking passengers for tea in the dining car. In the true tradition of a good headwaiter, he did not bat an eyelid as he stepped over a half-naked lady.

As the time approached to rendezvous with the car, we set up in the corridor and wondered if our gamble would pay off. Travelling at some sixty miles an hour, we approached the stretch of road and prayed that the car would be able to gain enough speed and keep up. A cheer went up as we came to the spot and saw the car. Later at the hotel, we discovered that they had exceeded the speed limit and had some difficulty gaining enough speed. It did not matter, the gamble had come off and the shot was perfect. It was definitely the highlight of the trip so far. Arrival in Milan at about 9.15 pm became potentially dramatic when we discovered that the baggage van containing our equipment was securely locked on the platform side, and resisted all attempts to open it. A decision was taken to send the crew ahead to the hotel, which hopefully they would reach before the restaurant closed at 11 pm. The assistant director and myself stayed behind with a self-drive van to follow later when we could get the equipment unloaded.

The call to send the crew ahead was to haunt me for many years to come. Why? Because, apart from my other responsibilities, I would have ensured the proper allocation of rooms. I do not know to this day if it was a wind up, but Nic told me that if he stood on a chair and peered out of a fanlight, he could just see the focus puller having breakfast on his balcony.

I find it hard to believe, but it has stuck with me to this day.

The next day was spent filming in and around the hotel including a sequence that involved Caroline sunbathing on the back of a speedboat on the lake. Unfortunately, we did not know that Caroline did not really like boats and lying out in a bikini for some two and a half hours in temperatures well into the eighties had a predictable effect. At 1 am, I was woken by Caroline's husband to say that she was very ill and would not be able to work that day. I habitually carried a number of standard remedies with me and the administration of some Kaolin and Morphine helped, but it was clear that the day's schedule would have to be changed to give her a very light workload. With only two days left, the original idea had been to shoot the final scene that day, and to change it meant using the hotel terrace on Saturday when it would be full of guests, including some well-known in the entertainment industry. We had planned a light last day as we had to be back in London that night and now we had to switch the schedule putting great pressure on everyone and putting our scheduled return in jeopardy.

Friday passed uneventfully, the local background artists were stood down and arrangements made with the hotel to shoot the final sequence on the final day, subject to the demands of other guests. Saturday dawned, and as the day progressed we set up to film the final reconciliation on the terrace that was gradually filling up. The hotel guests were very helpful and readily agreed to be seen in the background. I do not recall, but I suspect that, as usual, I picked up the bill for their drinks. By the afternoon, we were seriously worried about being finished and catching our plane to London. Yet again, I was very lucky and found that there was a later flight and was able to change our reservations.

We completed in time to catch the later flight and after getting everything through customs and paying the enormous excess baggage bill, I headed for the plane only to be stopped and searched by security who found I was carrying a Stanley knife. Fortunately, the security guard had never seen one and did not know how to open it. It was of course well before the strict security we go through today. We arrived in London at about 8.30 pm and filmed without incident on the following Monday to complete a highly successful shoot. One final twist to the story, ice melts in hot weather and plastic ice cubes are often used in photography. In this case, the agency had spent a substantial sum on replica cubes and we were on trust to return them safely. As we finished and rushed to pack, the barman did what he always did, and gathering up all the glasses emptied the remaining "ice" into the lake.

Presumably our very expensive ice is now "on the rocks" at the bottom of Lake Como.

I have written this from my own point of view, but it was of course a shining example of teamwork, and my thanks must go to the entire crew and agency team without whom we could never have met such a tight schedule. Finally, it has to be said that having Caroline's husband at the hotel proved a great advantage as it was he who looked after her and took a great deal of responsibility off my shoulders.

A very challenging job was to come my way when Jim was approached by the MD of an agency to make a commercial for a brand of cigars featuring an invisible man. I have to take it as a compliment that Jim immediately referred the problem to me. I looked into all the means of combining the image of the man (or rather his glasses and the cigar) with a live action background and interaction with other characters, but one by one dismissed all except one. We could not use a travelling matte as we could certainly not show smoke in that way and similarly any video effect would be unable to show him smoking the cigar.

In trying to arrive at the most satisfactory method of filming an invisible man, a number of techniques were explored and rejected. Front Projection, Travelling Matte, Pepe's Mirror and Videotape Chroma key all had problems when it came to losing the matte line completely. Not only this, but in order to support something as small as a cigar some sort of rigging was required. My conclusion was that we had to shoot everything for real and that we could not rely on special effects for any scene. There was only one way to achieve the perfect result and that was to create the scenes for real in camera. It would mean working with sheets of glass in a darkened studio with plenty of black velvet drapes. Any hint of reflection would destroy the illusion. This meant laying down detailed instructions for every scene and operating in a blacked out studio to control any reflection. In effect, I was going to have to direct the commercial. Two sheets of optically correct glass were used, one to portray the man in profile and the second to show a frontal close-up.

Two pairs of glasses were carefully mounted through the centre of the glass sheets, one mounted through the bridge for the profile shots, the other pair mounted with the lenses on the front surface with the ear pieces on the reverse side of the sheet. The story was to show our man checking into a hotel and being greeted not only by the receptionist with the line, "Nice to see you again." But also by two girls whose comment was, "Still smoking *those* cigars?" The hotel receptionist was played with his usual aplomb by John Savident, best known for his appearance as the butcher in *Coronation Street*. Some setups were simple. Picking up the key was simply a reversed shot and turning the register for signature just a matter of working it from below the desk. The one shot that I could not work out was how to get the pen out of its holder and across to the register for our man to sign in.

One evening on the train home to Haywards Heath, I suddenly came up with the solution. I had realised that in those days, most pens were made in two sections for inserting new ball point or ink cartridges, and as soon as I got home I went into my workshop and drilled a hole in a sheet of glass and assembled a pen with the nib on one side and the body of the pen on the other. Problem solved. On the shoot, I sat under the camera and carefully lifted my sheet of glass, transferred the two parts of the pen and began to write his name.

I was also instrumental in another key shot where our man was seen talking with the cigar in his mouth. We had a very good prop man on the unit, but the finest line that he had could not be attached to the cigar as it would be seen. As the set was blacked out, we had plenty of black nylon velvet. So I unravelled a piece producing a thread so fine that we could tie it around the cigar. Once again, I sat under the camera tweaking the cigar in time with his words. My director on this shoot was Mike Hodges, an experienced feature director, but this was a special effects film and he was happy for me to design each set up and go along with the restrictions placed on him by the technique. It was a very successful production, and I make no excuses. It involved special effects that I love, and I was certainly the only producer in the company with the knowledge and experience to pull it off! I have always believed in the saying that "there is no such thing as a problem, only a solution."

Flushed with our success, we were asked to shoot another commercial for the product. This time our man was to be seen checking in at an airport desk, a roughly similar situation. The managing director of the agency, Geers Gross, was not an easy man to please and on this production he sat and watched our rushes while we were still shooting on day two. He decided that he did not like something and phoned the studio and started complaining. I cannot remember what the problem was but we had not only the creative team but one of the directors of the agency in the studio all the time and his complaints seemed petty and unnecessary. The result was a meeting at the agency that Jim and I attended. I recall him having to restrain me when we were criticised in front of three members of the agency who had signed off on all we shot, but did not, or could not, speak up. They were being totally ignored. I believe the creative team left the agency soon after.

The variety of commercials shown on television has changed quite dramatically over the years. When television advertising started, there were not only the fifteen-, thirty-, and sixty-second spots that we are familiar with today, but also seven-second spots and advertising magazines. Among the magazines I particularly remember one, *Jim's Inn*, which was set in a pub with the landlord played by actor Jimmy Handley. Jimmy played a congenial host along with his wife Maggie and a succession of regulars would come to the bar and the conversation would turn to the latest lawn mower one had bought or the paint he had just used or some other product. The purpose of the magazine format, which ran for fifteen minutes, was to support smaller advertisers. There were several other Admags but none of them survived and *Jim's Inn* was by far the most successful lasting for some six years.

Over the years what is allowable in a commercial has also changed dramatically. Originally, one could advertise medical remedies that are no longer on the market, and were possibly of dubious effect. Today it seems that almost any product is acceptable, although I personally feel that some of the results are in very bad taste. Cars were not advertised on television for many years and I do not remember any bank advertising, whereas today they are two of the biggest spenders. Household products have always been in the forefront of advertisers and I have certainly made more than my fair share of their commercials, but cars and banks have also featured over the years. I have produced commercials for Barclays, Midland, and TSB and each in its own way presented unusual challenges.

For the Barclays commercial called *Money Man*, our actor had to be covered in pound notes. He had to wear a lightweight body suit to which the cash could be fixed. All very well but the adhesive being used started to overcome our man. A halt had to be called, but eventually he recovered and with the aid of coins for his eyes and in his mouth the commercial was completed. Years later, I was to work for Barclays again, this time in a commercial for South Africa. This was to provide me with a very different set of problems, but more of that later.

The TSB commercial highlighted their mortgages and we were asked to show an estate where one of the houses would be replaced by a mortgage deed. Yet again, this was well before the television techniques that would be used today, so we had to shoot on a real location and produce the effect on camera. This was to be my first experience of using a foreground matte painting. We selected a close just outside Croydon that had a grass recreation area in the centre of a crescent of typical suburban homes. We built a scaffolding tower in the grass area having first cleared our intentions with the householders in the close. The camera was set up for a shot of the houses and fixed in a locked off position, then a sheet of optical glass was secured in front of the camera and a very skilled specialist artist was able to paint the relevant document obscuring one of the houses. Great care had to be taken to avoid reflections and to ensure the camera and painting were rigidly fixed. The only other consideration was that there was sufficient light to ensure the required depth of focus between the painting and the background and, of course, pray it didn't rain. The shoot was a success but one resident (there is always one!) complained to the client about his house being in the commercial. The house concerned was not actually shown, or only on the very edge of screen. So really he had no grounds for complaint.

Some years later I was asked to produce another TSB commercial, this time it was not for mortgages but to promote them as "The bank that likes to say yes". It was a straightforward shoot that went very smoothly, but I felt that the agency, J. Walter Thompson, was missing a trick and should have ended the commercial with the obvious slogan: T "YES" B, and I told them so. The client changed agencies, and a year or so later a new commercial was on air using the slogan.

Perhaps the biggest challenge was to come when I was asked to bid on a commercial for Midland Bank business banking. The slogan was "We back business, we don't hold business back", and it was based on a *Gulliver's Travels* scenario. The agency wanted a particular director and I produced an initial estimate of something approaching half a million pounds. The agency took the project to another company, Avanti, ironically run by one of my ex-employees, and I thought that it was gone for good. I was surprised to get a call some weeks later to say that the agency was not happy with the company and wanted me to take on the project. The chosen director was on holiday abroad, so it was down to me to organise the production in his absence and then make sure that Jim Garrett got hold of him and got his agreement to shooting the storyboard that the team I had selected would produce. I called together a team who regularly worked with the director who was once again, Richard Loncraine. Art director, cameraman, editor and optical house technician, the agency producer and myself met and thrashed out a detailed storyboard and schedule.

It was now up to Jim.

This was to become my first production budget to exceed half a million pounds, but not the last. Richard accepted the challenge, and although he made his own contribution, completed a very successful shoot. The script called for a giant man to be seen being tied down by a group of miniature men who fired mortars with rope lines and gradually tied the giant down with stakes driven into the floor around him. The effect was achieved using a combination of giant set pieces, the bottom of a door, skirting, a table and, of course, a leg of our supposed giant. We only needed to build one leg as this was sufficient to show the ropes being tied down. We then cut to a wide shot of our actual man with the miniature characters in the foreground by the use of a split diopter, a lens allowing two differing-sized images to be photographed at the same time and a certain amount of optical work. At the appropriate time in the voice-over, our man is seen breaking free from his bonds with graphic shots of the stakes being pulled from the floor and ropes being pulled apart to coincide with the commentary saying. "…we don't hold business back." Over all, it was pretty much a classic example of how pre-planning could achieve a very dramatic effect with a minimum amount of construction, building only just enough to achieve the effect, and no more.

A producer has to be many things, above all, perhaps, a negotiator and co-ordinator of input from several different – and often opposing – sources. The first thing is to produce a budget to make the commercial to the agency brief and usually with input from the director, who will probably have been chosen by the agency producer. In many cases, my directors were from the feature world and had strong views, but where I found myself working with young or inexperienced directors, in commercial terms, I saw it as my responsibility to back them up by making sure they had the most suitable crew for the job. In other words, I would cast the crew just as we would cast the actors.

Having had to work with other people's inadequate budgets in the early days and frequently being put in the invidious position of having to ask the client for more money, I vowed that I would never ask for additional sums unless it was for some last-minute change the agency or client had made. So once a budget was agreed, it was down to me to make sure the project was delivered on budget, and on time. This meant ensuring the director was kept under control and did what I wanted him to do. Perhaps an over simplification, but that is how it was in practice. I had a particular view of my job and liked to think of myself as the agency and client's representative in the production company, with the agency producer having a complementary role. I was, after all, in the advertising business, not the film business and if I had a contribution to make, I was not afraid to make it. Perhaps it was, this attitude that led to one of my ex-clients including the following quote about me in a recent book, "A producer who had listened to both agency and client needs...he was the consummate professional, one of the few who made this business work."

I have already talked about my close relationship with Harry Sheppard of Marks & Spencer, who simply did not get on with his agency, but there have been many other examples of my involvement with clients and agencies over creative matters. I mentioned how my experience helped reduce the budget in year three for Black and Decker, but I was also involved closely with the animation sequences for the Heinz "Souperday" series. After the live action start, there was an animated insert to cover the jingle, "It's a Heinz Souperday". The agency producer went on holiday and I was in the agency for a meeting to discuss two options.

One option was for rather metallic lettering that the agency was favouring, while option two was for a much more flowing and softer approach that I felt was more suitable. I argued my case effectively and won the day. It may have been at that point that I gained the respect of the Creative Director, Dennis Auton of Y&R, who I came to know very well. Years later he invited me into the agency projection box as they presented to the client the latest commercials for Double Diamond that I had produced. The commercials were well received but the client decided to move the account. Dennis then wrote me a personal letter explaining that it was absolutely nothing to do with the commercials, and that he took full responsibility. Apparently the client had fallen out with the agency when in a previous job, and was in effect, getting his own back.

My relationship with Procter & Gamble could not have been stronger. When I ran my own company and executives came over from head office in Cincinnati, they were put in touch with me and not infrequently I was asked to arrange theatre tickets and I became known as the Keith Prowse of Curzon Street.

From time to time, I became involved in producing music videos, working with Richard Lester was an obvious connection to The Beatles, and particularly Paul McCartney, but Michael Lindsay-Hogg was also a connection and it was through him that I became the producer of the original *Mull of Kintyre* promo and that was some exercise and one of the most DIY jobs I have ever undertaken. The first thing to do was to visit the location. That meant flying from London to Glasgow and taking a small plane to Machrihanish, near Campbeltown. At London Airport there was a flight delay of two hours due to fog and it was then that I discovered that my director was terrified of flying. So having checked with the airline, I suggested we go to a local hotel for a drink. On returning in plenty of time for our flight, we were told it had left. There was only one thing to do, so we headed for Euston Station and managed to get on an overnight train to Glasgow. We got our morning flight in a plane of about ten seats and started to look for a suitable location. Looking along the shoreline we saw a tower – quite possibly a folly – that seemed to offer a good background. We found that the area was owned by an elderly couple who had a house not far inland.

We approached the house and were invited in, and not for the first or last time, I was amazed at people's hospitality as we were offered lunch. We explained our quest, and despite some reservations over Paul's connection with cannabis, we were given the go-ahead. So after establishing contact with the local hotel and the general store in Campbeltown, it was back to London. The budget was small so the production became something of an exercise in self-sufficiency. I brought in an assistant director who had previously worked for my company and together we hired a Land Rover and trailer which we filled with a substantial marquee and enough cooking equipment to cater not only for ourselves but the entire Campbeltown pipe band and a host of extras from the local community. It was about 1 pm when Peter Dolman and I set off for Kintyre from my office in Queen Street, Mayfair.

By 10 pm we were in Glasgow and collected some fish and chips for supper before continuing to Campbeltown in what was fast becoming very unpleasant weather. Fortunately, by the time we reached our hotel at something like 1.30 am, the thunderstorm we had driven through had abated and we were able to get a few hours of badly needed sleep.

The next morning, we were aided by locals as we struggled in still windy weather to erect our marquee. We had arranged for the food supplies to come from the Campbeltown store and duly set up our kitchen that was to be operated by local ladies. We were to shoot the following day and were joined by the rest of the unit, mainly recruited from the local film crews available in Glasgow. We filmed on the beach and with the Campbeltown pipe band and in particular the Pipe Major. We were grateful for good weather during the shoot and all went well.

The promo was to end with a scene of villagers gathering round a bonfire on the beach at night and this presented something of a challenge as, in view of a very limited budget, I had only brought up from London two electricians with a Land Rover generator and one Brute, (an arc light). This was deployed to illuminate the aforesaid tower in the background, while the foreground and crowd were to be seen by light from the bonfire. There were not a lot of Health and Safety regulations in those days and in any case we were well away from any public area so it became a very DIY operation. I had taken with me a small chainsaw and this enabled the building of a substantial bonfire, but how to get enough light for filming? The solution was both simple and probably dangerous as I, out of camera shot, added several doses of paraffin to the already blazing fire. It worked and that was all that mattered. I have one more lasting memory of the shoot having been told off by Linda for trying to kill a wasp that was surveying her lunch. I subsequently produced other promos for McCartney including *London Town*. There was also one with Elton John and one shot in New York with The Rolling Stones.

Working on government-backed projects meant working through the C.O.I., the Central Office of Information, and I worked with them on several occasions, for road safety, motorcycle helmet safety, the sale of council houses and other projects, one of which for road safety in Northern Ireland deserves more than a quick mention. The C.O.I. being a government department had strict controls over budgets and I believe the markup that we were allowed in those far off days was 10% as opposed to the commercially accepted 25% – 30%. In addition, you were allowed a profit of 2.5 %. I have already mentioned that the production estimate form that I developed over time became, along with that developed by another producer, the industry standard and it all began with the C.O.I. Quite simply, by putting more and more detailed items in the estimate before markup, one was able to achieve a reasonable profit.

I applied the same thinking to my work with Procter & Gamble, who originally had a system requiring a very short and incomplete breakdown of costs. I would not use their system and provided much more than they were asking for. One of my C.O.I. projects was to support the sale of council houses under the Thatcher government and it used a phrase that is today used by one of our major DIY retailers..."Make your house a home." The idea was to show a family in a home setting in a typical two-storey suburban home. This home was to be constructed in a studio without any outside walls, in other words, the first floor had to be cantilevered, or suspended, in some way as the children would be seen in a bedroom. We were told that it was impossible, but insisted we could do it, and we did. Having shot this sequence with a fixed camera position, the scene would change to the exterior shot of the house taken by a stills photographer on a housing estate from a matching angle.

Now for the biggest job I ever undertook for the C.O.I. It was for Road Safety in Northern Ireland, and was to be shot on location, despite the troubles at the time. Apparently, the number of road deaths was unacceptably high compared with other areas of the UK and it had been decided to produce a specifically local campaign rather than show the current mainland advertising, despite the fact that a very high proportion of the budget would have to be spent on production. We all enjoy a joke from time to time but some nationalities come in for more than their fair share of ridicule. Sometimes though it seems that it could be based on fact. On our first recce trip, the young director and I were to find out just how much the commercials were needed.

The Northern Ireland Office allocated a liaison officer to us who proved to be a somewhat daring driver. On more than one occasion we counted ourselves lucky not to have become the subject of one of our own commercials. White lines were regarded as a challenge, lights as something to be beaten and corners were largely disregarded, and even NO ENTRY signs could be ignored. We were soon to discover that this was only the beginning of our education. I was told that if I wanted to see an employee before 8 am, I would be well advised to keep him up all night. It certainly seemed that our Irish drivers could not tell the time and phrases like, "I didn't know you could read a newspaper by daylight at eight o'clock in the morning," or "I never knew that seven o'clock existed," became a standing joke. Messages or instructions were never passed on, or if they were, it would be to someone who had nothing whatever to do with the matter in hand.

We were working with an Irish advertising agency that had written scripts featuring a local nurse and a police officer speaking to camera in addition to scenic shots of the province and finally a staged road accident. There were a number of locations to be found including a hospital, sections of road where we could film in relative safety and another section where we could stage the crash complete with crashed vehicles, police, ambulance and fire engine. Finding the locations was not too much of a problem, various tourist scenes from Newcastle in the south to the Giant's Causeway in the north were obvious from the start and gave us a chance to visit the famous Bushmills Distillery! Our liaison officer found a stretch of dual carriageway that had not yet been handed over by the contractor and that completed our location search. So far so good, but it was not to last.

Casting was very important and we were presented with a police officer and a staff nurse who had already been selected. We were very happy with the choice of police officer but less so with the nurse, who had been chosen on the basis of rank rather than personality or acting ability. The director and I both felt that we needed someone younger and more extroverted. We were, after all, appealing to a younger audience and needed to get the message home. We decided we had to recast and with this in mind went to a large hospital where we seated ourselves in the nurses' recreation room and surveyed the passing talent. It was a difficult job but someone had to do it! As a succession of young nurses came in for a coffee break, it was soon apparent who we should approach. I do not remember either of us ever saying, "We can get you on TV," but that was indeed the gist of the conversation. We were looking for a young nurse who was an extrovert, chatty and fun, as we felt this would give us the best chance of finishing filming without our nurse getting stage fright. The attractive and vivacious young nurse we selected agreed to do the job if she could bring her friend with her to which we saw no objection.

Unfortunately, that was where we made our first mistake, they were both trainees and would have to be portrayed as qualified nurses and we had not consulted matron! Help had to come from the Northern Ireland Office in order to overcome the objections and in due course the two nurses were suitably attired in new uniforms. Problem number one solved.

A key part of a producer's job is to schedule the filming in the most economical way and on this occasion there were scenic shots that did not involve either sound or lighting and could be completed on the first day (a Monday), while the generator electricians and sound crew were travelling from London having avoided the weekend.

Another part of the job is to promote the right atmosphere amongst crew and artistes, particularly where non-professional artistes are concerned and to this end I arranged a dinner party for the Sunday evening before the shoot to which I invited our two nurses and the policeman and his wife. Everyone turned up at our hotel on time but very quickly our nurse told us that she could not do the job. Apparently matron had forbidden her to do so and was sending someone more senior in her place.

Problem number two and we had not yet started.

We told her that matron did not have the power to overrule the Northern Ireland Office or indeed to tell us how to make commercials. We reassured her that we would deal with matron in the morning and she was not to worry. The evening went very well and having said farewell to our guests we retired to bed, the camera crew was scheduled to set off at 7 am to shoot the pictorial scenes while I arranged to go to Stormont to seek help in dealing with matron. Having to pull rank on her I was praying that I would not end up in one of her wards!

We all assembled for breakfast at 6.30 am and the two local minibuses arrived to take the crew and rendezvous on the front in Newcastle. All seemed well as I saw them both off before returning to finish a good breakfast. It was just as well that I could not go to Stormont before 9 am as at around 7.45 am the first minibus returned having lost its way and found itself passing the hotel again. As it happened, the cameraman had left something behind so it could be regarded as fortuitous, though hardly a good omen for the rest of the shoot.

Problem number three.

Having seen them on their way for the second time, I felt sure we were finally getting our act together, but I was wrong. Half an hour later the other driver was on the phone having forgotten where to rendezvous with the first minibus.   Was this yet another sign of things to come?

Problem number four and we had still not started.

Problem number five was soon to emerge as I later discovered. One of our drivers had failed to fill up before setting out despite a specific instruction to the contrary. Having announced that he had to return to his base to get petrol, it had to be pointed out that there were places called garages where one could buy petrol. The assistant director paid up but by now confidence in our transport company was at an all time low. My visit to Stormont was uneventful, matron was eventually placated and my cast restored. By the end of the day, I was waiting for the return of the crew and a report of the day's events when I heard about the petrol incident, which incidentally was to happen to me with another driver later in the week.

The rest of the crew arrived from London and we all had a good laugh, but secretly wondered what would happen next. We did not have long to wait!   Having finished filming at a hospital on the Tuesday shortly before lunch, we were to move to another location and having some loose ends to tie up I remained behind when the unit drove off. "Don't worry, sir," the driver said. "I'll be back within half an hour." Two hours later I was still waiting and in those days there were no mobile phones and we had no walkie-talkies, even if they would have been able to make contact.

Problem number six.

Day three dawned and the time came for our nurse to deliver her lines while driving a Mini. The transport company had been briefed to ensure that the car had been serviced and was running smoothly as it was important for sound quality. The camera was rigged on the car, the lines rehearsed to the director's satisfaction and the car moved off with a rather ominous rattle. Within half a mile the exhaust blew and sound recording became virtually impossible.

Round seven to the Irish.

The fourth day, Thursday, (you will see the relevance of my mentioning this in a moment) and we had to stage our crash scene at night on our newly completed section of road that was still owned by the contractors. We had arranged for two newly crashed cars to be supplied by our somewhat suspect transport company and I had been personally assured that they would not be rusty and that the petrol tanks would have been drained. The scene was set, crashed vehicle on its side, all emergency vehicles in attendance, flashing lights and our police officer and nurse ready to deliver their advice to the driving public. All went surprisingly well and we finished shooting just after midnight.

All well? I should have known better! When the last car was lifted onto its low loader it became apparent that the petrol tank had not been properly drained and had emptied itself onto the newly laid road surface. Anyone who has ever had the misfortune to get covered in tar on a beach will know that a good way of removing it is with petrol and our car had left a gaping hole in the road surface. The contractor was none too pleased and threatened to sue, but as it was a government project agreed to sort it out.

Round eight to the Irish, we were not doing well.

I mentioned that it was Thursday and the relevance of this is that we were due to fly back to London at the end of filming the next day, Friday. Union rules stated that the crew must be given a ten-hour break between calls and as we were not back at the hotel before 1 am, it meant an 11 am start for the last sequence before catching our flight back at 5 pm. Unfortunately, we had lost a couple of hours due to weather earlier in the week and needed to start again at 9 am, it meant that the unit would be paid at overtime rates for the first two hours, known as time off the clock.

They would then be paid continuously until they arrived home. So, with two hours overtime to start the day, it was important to finish as early as possible to ensure catching our flight before the overtime became punitive. We did not have our own catering truck and had so far eaten pretty well at local hostelries but all that was about to change! We were some thirty miles outside Belfast and there were no facilities in the area so we did what we always did in those circumstances, and sent one of our drivers to get whatever he could from the nearest village or town. It was assumed that he would be back in about forty minutes at the most but no, after an hour and a half (and a further hour on the overtime bill for a lost meal break) he returned and proudly presented his purchases. Hungry as they were, I don't think anyone ate what was on offer which was basically congealed fish and chips looking very sorry for itself. Somehow it did not seem to matter that there was only enough for half the unit in any case.

Was I right in thinking that our driver had found his own lunch? Wasn't there a whiff of Guinness in the air?

It was certainly round nine to the Irish.

By four o'clock filming was completed and we packed up and headed off to catch the 5 pm shuttle to Heathrow. So far so good, but yet again I should have known better! Tired and hungry, we joined the throng of other passengers in the terminal building, the airport was fogbound and closed. There was no food available, no planes and precious little information. By nine o'clock, we were getting pretty angry and fed up with British Airways, the weather and the Irish. Two members of the crew had flights out of London the next morning and I had seven cars and a camera truck waiting for us at Heathrow. After some fairly heated exchanges with the airline duty officer, we were told that a plane was expected at 10 pm and that we would be given seats. Unfortunately we were told that our one and a half tons of equipment could not go with us. More angry scenes were followed by threats as to what the Northern Ireland Minister to whom we were answerable would say when his commercials were not delivered on time.

We were, in fact, on a very tight schedule and expecting to start editing over the weekend. The assistant director was, to put it politely, f-o-r-c-e-f-u-l. And gave the duty officer a piece of his mind. How it happened I don't know but somehow we found ourselves taking the equipment with us to the aircraft and somehow it all got loaded. Considering the incredibly tight security on any flight from Belfast, it was something of a miracle as none of it was inspected and I can only assume that our threat of retribution from the Northern Ireland Office must have taken effect.

One effect of the security was that my cashbox and petty cash had to go in the hold and a box of miniature bottles of whiskey the director had bought for the crew had to be emptied and distributed. It seemed to make little sense as we had loaded our own equipment unchecked.

Was this one point to the English?

Being a shuttle flight, we knew that there was no food or drink service on board and all we could get was water to go with our miniature whiskies. As we left the ground, I am quite sure other members of the crew felt as I did, a sense of relief at finally leaving a place where nothing could be taken at face value. We were dozing fitfully when we were woken by the captain's voice. We may have thought that we had escaped but the Irish had one more trump card and it was an ace.

"Ladies and gentlemen," came the captain's voice, "I am sorry to tell you that there is a bomb scare at Heathrow and the airport is closed, we have plenty of fuel on board so we are going to circle until the control tower reopens. The weather is not very good, but this plane is equipped for a blind landing in bad weather so it should not present a problem." For perhaps forty minutes we circled before the captain addressed us again, "Ladies and gentlemen, your captain again, the control tower has reopened, but I'm afraid the weather is now so bad that we are unable to land and are diverting to Manchester." It was now well past midnight and I don't think anything would have surprised us at this stage. The crew was probably thinking of the overtime they were earning and where to go on holiday. I was thinking of all the vehicles still at Heathrow.

It must have been about 1.30 in the morning when we finally touched down in Manchester and taxied to a halt. Nothing much happened for some time until the captain's voice came over the loudspeaker yet again. "Very sorry about this, ladies and gentlemen, but it seems there are no steps available to get you off the aircraft. I am told it could be up to an hour and a half before we can disembark. Cabin crew I suggest you open the doors and (clearly as frustrated as we were and breaking every safety rule) those of you who wish to smoke may do so."

In fact, we were lucky and were off the plane in just over thirty minutes and after checking all the equipment off the conveyor we all sat on the camera cases wondering what on earth could befall us next. At this point we were given our first food since breakfast on the previous day, a sandwich that had clearly been at the airport a great deal longer than we had. I, of course, was desperately trying to find some means of getting us to London. The transport at Heathrow would have got the message by now but how and when would we eventually arrive? All efforts failed. There were no trains available, no coaches, busses, not even a pantechnicon, and I returned to dozing uncomfortably among the equipment. Eventually at about 5.30 am, we were told a coach had been found which would take us to Crewe from where we could catch a train to London.

Wearily we picked up the equipment again and loaded it into the coach and I followed my crew on board clutching a bunch of first class tickets. Once on the platform at Crewe, I organised a party to load the equipment into the guard's van while others, including myself, were detailed to find seats. A train arrived and it was a sight for genuinely tired eyes. After a day without food and a night without sleep, especially having worked outside the previous day, we must have looked a pretty rough bunch.

I made a beeline for a first class compartment which already contained two elderly male passengers. As I burst in, one of them looked over his newspaper and said rather aggressively, "This is a first class compartment." I had had enough and thrusting my handful of tickets at him, for the first time in my life, I swore at a member of the public, "AND THESE ARE F**KING FIRST CLASS TICKETS!" Just as well he was not Irish or I might have strangled him.

We arrived at Euston at about 9 am and were met by the drivers that had been reorganised by my office and I eventually reached home in Sussex at midday, some twenty-seven hours after starting work on Friday morning. It was, of course, now the weekend and overtime rates were not only doubled but an additional day had to be added for the lost night. The crew earned a fortune, but I was not on overtime and did not appreciate the joke.

I found myself being asked to produce a commercial for America with Andre Agassi, presumably because he was in the UK at the time. The ad was for a Peugeot car, or as the Americans called it, a Poo Jo. A location was found on an exclusive estate in Surrey where the houses were set back with sweeping lawns and no fences, so they looked reasonably like the U.S. The location was not a problem but the car was, it had been imported and was not registered and to add to the problem only ran on unleaded petrol that was not available in the UK. Who was it who said, "there are no problems, only solutions?" Whoever it was would have made a good producer and the problems were solved with the cooperation of our insurers and a limited amount of lead-free petrol was produced. Another successful exercise.

I mentioned that my company had, very unusually, won an award for an Ajax floor cleaning commercial. The producer of that commercial was a young lady working at that time for an agency known as NCK. Her name was Sheena McCoy. We became friends and I was to work with her several more times when she worked at FCB, and latterly at JWT, where she had been employed by my old friend, Mike Gilmour, on my recommendation.

At FCB, she asked me to produce a commercial for Ferguson television sets, featuring the famous conductor, André Previn. I produced commercials with Previn for the next three years. Most of the commercials were very straightforward and were remembered mainly for the arrival just before lunch on each shoot of his family. One shoot, I believe the last in the series, was rather different. The script called for a studio set through the windows of which a moving cloud background was seen. My director was Mike Hodges, and our cameraman one of those with a good showreel (probably because he had worked with Ridley Scott), and absolutely no technical knowledge whatsoever. To achieve the background effect we were using a tried and tested method of back projection in which the cloudscape was projected by a projector linked by a three-phase supply to the camera onto a translucent screen.

The camera was set in a fixed position and the background film checked. The camera was a reflex one which meant that the background scene was recorded as the shutter rotated in between the times when it was open to record the foreground scene. Ensuring synchronisation of background and foreground images meant that it was important that the operator did not see any background image through the viewfinder. The shoot went well and we all anticipated a good set of rushes the following morning. But we were to get a rather nasty shock, not one frame of the background had been captured.

I questioned the cameraman as he had operated the shot himself in view of the importance of getting it right. "I had a perfect picture in the viewfinder," he said. I nearly exploded. "Don't you realise it is a reflex camera and you should have seen nothing!" I replied. I was paying this man nearly a thousand pounds for a day's work and he had no idea how his equipment works. This was something I came across on more than one occasion and it resulted from the too rapid growth of the industry and total lack of training.

Yes, I could have looked through the camera myself, but that is not something a producer normally does and when I have done it in the past there have been comments in the crew. Apparently, producers are not supposed to be technicians and at his salary level I could at least have expected him to know how a camera worked. All was not quite lost as we had more work to do and it was a two-day shoot so we were able to shoot the sequence again the following day, although it did cause us some overtime and I could not believe it when the cameraman put in his claim.

Some time during my run of Ferguson commercials, I was approached by the Ferguson company and offered the job of heading up a new unit to market video discs. Whether or not it would have been today's DVDs, I do not know, but they were offering a six-month contract at substantially less than I was earning at the time. It was, of course, Sheena who had put me forward but I am afraid that my reply was that it would have been tantamount to signing on as a deck chair attendant on the *Titanic*.

I was to produce several beer commercials for the American market and one in particular comes to mind. I was familiar with the agency producer and his creative team and with their blessing he was going to direct. It was the launch commercial for a new product and it was claiming to have been developed from an ancient recipe originating in a monastery. The agency had a London office and the director contacted them and took their advice on the choice of cameraman. My recommendation was rejected and the consequence was another disaster story of ending up with someone who had a good showreel due far more to the fact that he had worked with good directors than his own talent, as you will see.

The location was to be an abbey with several monks dressed virtually in sackcloth habits seen in a storeroom where the barrels were kept when the bishop is driven through the gatehouse in his coach and comes to the open door. We managed to assemble a cast of monks from quite well-known character actors and sort out the problems of payment for the American market. Next the location, and we settled on Cleve Abbey in Somerset. It was winter and it was going to be cold shooting in the ruined Abbey. On the recce, I took my clients to a fifteenth-century pub for lunch. It had originally been part of the Abbey complex, but had long since become a classic country pub. There was a roaring log fire in the inglenook, several dogs sprawled around and, in American eyes, a traditional English scene. Anticipating my clients' next question, I enquired about accommodation and yes it was available. The shoot was set up and the weather got colder. Our clients got their wish and the crew and artistes were spread over two conventional hotels in Minehead. The results were, I suppose, predictable, the clients had draughty rooms, little hot water and no telephones in the rooms, while we were warm in our modest, but modern, accommodation.

To get back to the choice of cameraman, he demanded three brutes, very large carbon arc lights each needing two electricians. The lights could not be used inside the building and were simply used to indicate sunlight coming in through the openings in the walls where at one time there might have been windows. That was fair enough although rather over the top but it meant a strong light coming into the room from behind our cast and the shadows fell accordingly towards the camera.

We then cut to a reverse shot as the bishop arrived in the entrance. Once again our cameraman set the strong light behind the bishop as he came forward – he had little option with only his chosen huge lights. The light was so strong that not only were the shadows thrown forward but as he reached the doorway, his head actually disappeared. That was not all, after more than an hour, he had to admit that he could not light a glass of beer. I had to do that in a small studio in Soho when we got back. By way of explanation, liquid in a glass cannot be photographed however much light you use you can only light through it so you will usually have a piece of silver or gold card placed strategically behind the glass or another light source of some kind through which the glass passes if it is a moving shot.

215

When I was shooting a Double Diamond commercial, our actor was being seen from the end of a pub bar and had to raise the glass and drink. As it is a tricky shot, and our actor had to be very precise with his movement, I instructed the camera operator to cut the shot if the glass did not pass through the light source fixed at the far end of the bar. This was to stop the shot before the actor started drinking for obvious reasons. The Double Diamond was an important contract for the company and Jim Garrett turned up at the studio just as this scene was about to be shot. The first three takes were NG and my operator cut as asked. Jim turned to me and said, "I do not want to see that operator on any of our jobs in future." He was one of the very best commercial operators in the business and I continued to work with him for many years.

It was not to be the first time I ignored or overruled my chairman.

A year after the Cleve Abbey shoot, I was asked to produce a follow-up commercial with the same team. This time the script called for the monks to be seen in rather more conventional settings and the chosen locations were Leeds Castle where we chose Edward I's wine cellar, and a cellar room at Ightham Mote and finally an exterior scene at a monastery in Spain near Alicante. This time I had my choice of cameraman accepted and I also arranged rather more suitable accommodation.

When I arranged with the custodian to film at Leeds Castle, he suggested that as there were no other events taking place and it would not involve employing more staff, we might like to stay there. The agency members were, of course, responsible for their own living expanses and I could not afford to pay for them out of the budget, so I agreed that they would pass over to me their per diem allowances for the two days that we would be at the Castle and accepted the offer. My clients flew into London on a Sunday and I arranged for them to be picked up and brought straight to the Castle. Shirley and I had arrived earlier, my wife being slightly taken aback when the butler's first words to her were, "Shall I unpack for you, madam?" Thinking quickly of the haste with which she had packed, and the Marks & Spencer contents of the case, she declined his offer.

The clients duly arrived and were shown into the sitting room where we were already installed before the log fire. Shortly, the butler was to bring us afternoon tea with cucumber sandwiches. I had arranged dinner that evening and asked the custodian and his wife to join us. We assembled in the library for pre-dinner drinks before being shown into the dining room as the butler announced that dinner was served.

I had chosen the menu and the wines and we ate and drank very well. I do not remember the whole menu but I do remember that the fish course was Dover sole in a champagne sauce. This will give you some idea of the scale of the event.

At the end of the two days I had to leave the unit in the care of the assistant director whom I knew well and had worked with for several years. He was more than capable of taking the camera crew to complete the exterior establishing shots of the monastery in Spain. I was due to fly to Johannesburg that day for a Sunsilk shampoo shoot. All went well until the plane to Alicante was diverted to Madrid where all the equipment had to be unloaded as customs rules dictate that all goods have to be cleared at the point of entry into the country. This was unexpected and neither our customs officer nor the local contact were there, meanwhile I was blissfully unaware on my flight to South Africa.

On arrival in Johannesburg, I went straight to our local office who had set up casting sessions and location recce for myself and the director, Catherine Lefevre, one of two French directors I found myself working with at the time. Catherine arrived overnight from Paris on the Friday straight into two days of intensive pre-production. The schedule for the Sunsilk production was tight and I had already had to fly to New York by Concorde with the agency producer to hold casting sessions there as hair commercials were notoriously difficult to cast. At one of our sessions we saw Jerry Hall. The client, Unilever, had contracted the high-profile London hair stylist, Leonard of Mayfair, as the hairdresser for the productions and presumably his testimony, and he arrived with a case full of hair products that needed some explaining to the bemused South African customs officers. After all, that was the time of apartheid and we were dealing with an organisation that banned the book *Black Beauty* on racial grounds! Our shoot went well, but we did have a rainstorm that kept us in our vehicles at Hartbeespoort Dam. We were parked a short distance from a snake park and a snack bar and for those of us with the courage we had our first taste of snake.

I was to work with Catherine again on another two clashing projects, in fact, she had made a point of trying to ensure that I was always her producer, much to Jim Garrett's annoyance. This time she was the director of both and it was a very serious clash, with one shoot in Los Angeles, which was extremely important to our New York office, and one for a South African agency to take place in London scheduled for the same week. The matter was made worse because the South African project, which was for Barclays Bank, had been secured by Jim himself on a trip to SA and he had given his word that the director would be available with plenty of time for pre-production and shooting on those particular dates.

At the same time, the managing director of our company in New York was about to take on another project for Dubonnet that was crucially important to the agency in Chicago, starring as it did the wife of the owner of the brand in the U.S., Pia Zadora, a young singer. Catherine was a very strong-willed lady, a trait that set her at odds with Jim when she tried to insist that I produced all her work for the company. As the clash became apparent, Jim decided that we had to pull out of the American job and I was dispatched on a Sunday to meet with the agency on the Monday morning in Chicago and pull out of the production. I was not able to talk to Catherine who was at the time filming in Hawaii and would only join us at the meeting next morning. Not for the first time, Jim had completely misjudged Catherine's reaction.

On the Monday, I went into the agency with the full intention of pulling the company out of the project.

Catherine's flight was delayed, but when she joined the meeting it quickly became apparent that she had no intention of giving up the job. The meeting was perfectly amicable, but I was helpless when my colleague signed the contract in front of me. What was I to do? The productions were scheduled to run on consecutive days, but one in L.A. and one in London. There was no alternative, I had to phone London with the news, a call I was not looking forward to. Somehow both productions had to go ahead and both clients had to be assured that they would get the service they had been promised.

By the end of the call I was under no illusion that it was all down to me and despite having flown to Chicago dressed for cold weather, I booked my flight to Los Angeles for that evening and booked into my favourite hotel, the Westwood Marquis. The Tuesday and Wednesday were spent preparing the Dubonnet shoot and attending a pre-production meeting with the agency. On the Thursday, Catherine flew back to Paris while the sets were being built. I had managed to have the shoot in L.A. delayed by one day that would give us just enough time to hold the pre-production meeting with the South African clients and keep them happy. They were due to arrive on Monday morning. I had already arranged casting sessions and booked an excellent art director who had produced very detailed set designs.

Catherine flew in on Monday morning and we had our first meeting. Casting and pre-production took up the next two days, but by the time the cast had been agreed, and they had been issued with cassettes of the

Afrikaans dialogue to learn as the commercial was to be shot in two languages, there was little left for the agency to do. I suggested that they took the next two days off to go sightseeing and prayed that they would not realise that I was sending their director back to Los Angeles.

By this time I had booked into a hotel as it was imperative that I stayed close to my director if I was to keep all the balls in the air. I had already called in a doctor who gave her injections of vitamins to keep her awake. Catherine flew back to L.A. on the first flight on the Thursday taking advantage of the eight-hour time difference to go straight to the studio for a rehearsal before filming on the Friday and Saturday. She then flew back to London overnight on the Sunday arriving just in time for a final day of preparation before shooting the Barclays commercial on the Tuesday and Wednesday. Somehow we had got through it and completed both shoots on time and with happy clients.

Jim was never one to offer any praise or thanks and nobody in the company made any comment. The Barclays agency team on the other hand presented me with a very fine bottle of vintage claret with thanks for a very smooth and successful production.

In 1977, I was appointed to the board of the company, but it was in name only and for Jim's benefit, not mine. I was also put into a company pension scheme but again it was probably run for Jim rather than any employee. Not once in some fifteen years was there ever a review and there was no advice on tax savings that could have been made by increasing contributions as I discovered

221

to my cost when I was eventually made redundant. Basically, with proper advice, I would now be living on a much larger pension.

It was in 1977 that Chrysler UK decided to launch a new small hatchback to be known as the Chrysler Sunbeam. The agency was Grant Advertising with offices in Basil Street alongside Harrods. The Creative Director was Richard Truman, a Canadian, who has written a book called *Mods, Minis and Madmen* in which he describes the progress of the production from the agency side in great detail, although I think perhaps there was a certain amount of exaggeration. My involvement came when the company was approached to bid on the commercial with director, Richard Lester. It was clear that we were in competition for what was going to be a very important shoot and one that could well influence the future of the company. The star of the commercial was to be Petula Clark.

The director, Dick Clement, with whom I had produced the Triumph commercial at Garretts, had left the company by this time but one of his last productions had been for our New York office, a household linen company featuring Petula Clark. So he seemed the obvious choice. Dick had formed his own production company with his writing partner, Ian La Frenais, called Witzend Productions. I was naturally concerned that Dick would be a natural choice for the job having recently worked with Petula, who was now being approached for the Chrysler ad. I had a conversation with Jim about the situation and contacted Dick offering him ten thousand pounds cash to come back and direct the commercial through us. He turned down the offer, preferring to promote his own production company that he had set up with his writing partner Ian La Frenais and Alan Mckeon, an ex-Garretts producer. I was eventually the winner of the contest and we duly got the job with Richard Lester directing.

This was the start of a series of episodes where I found myself in competition with Witzend over the next few years. I was bidding against them on two major American accounts, Ford with Jackie Stewart and programme openings and tags for Mobil Oil with Peter Ustinov. I won on every occasion and that prompted retaliation when suddenly the union appeared on the scene when I was filming in the wartime cabinet offices in Whitehall. They had clearly been tipped off as no one else could have known the location which was, of course, underground.

The agency, Richard Lester, and myself went to meet Petula at the Hôtel Plaza Athénée in Paris and subsequently set up the shoot. The idea was that Petula would be seen driving the car on her way to a TV performance. There was a music track that had been composed by Gus Galbraith and had received Petula's blessing. The words of the song were "Put a little sunbeam in your life", and for the commercial they were changed to "Put a Chrysler Sunbeam in your life". The shoot was fairly hectic with two assistants scouting in front of the unit and one Sussex policeman with us but all went well. My biggest problem was that when we got to the TV station where Petula was to be seen on stage, I had three camera crews, the film crew covering the television crew and a documentary unit covering all of us. Sorting out the fees with the shop stewards was quite a challenge.

Travel had become an essential part of my work and I enjoyed many overseas locations. Over the years I developed reliable contacts in many foreign locations, New Zealand, New York, Los Angeles, and San Francisco in America, South Africa and several European countries, most notably France, Spain and Italy. After years as a producer I was confident that if I had a conversation with a potential contact in most countries I could tell if we were talking the same language and they knew what they were doing.

When Sir Freddie Laker launched the first budget airline, I flew to Los Angeles with a film crew for a small amount of money. Subsequently, I flew with People Express, and eventually Virgin. By using Virgin in the early days, I was able to fly upper class as cheaply as club class on British Airways. The union dictated the class of travel for the crew according to the length of the flight, but only Jim always travelled first class on company business. I did learn one or two tricks, one of which was that if I was bringing back exposed film I would be paying excess baggage, but by upgrading to first class I avoided the extra charge.

One particular day of travelling will stay in my mind forever and I doubt if it can be matched. Catherine, our

French director and I were due to attend a meeting in Los Angeles, but she had a commitment in Paris before lunch and was not free for an early morning flight. I was picked up by my regular driver from home in Sussex and taken to the office where I spent a couple of hours before being taken to Heathrow where I had lunch before catching a flight to Paris. Meeting up with Catherine, we caught the afternoon Concorde to Washington where we had a three hour wait before our flight to L.A. was due to leave. We took a taxi and had a tour of the town. I don't remember what time we eventually arrived at the Westwood Marquis, but as we were shown into our two two-bedroom suite, Catherine looked at me as though to say, "Not tonight!" It may have been my imagination, but there was no way I could ever have fancied her.

Forty years ago music promos were in their infancy, budgets were not high and most were studio shoots and were not a patch on the elaborate end effects driven productions that they were to become. They were not an important part of our business, and I suspect they came through various director's contacts. *Mull of Kintyre* was the exception and I made more studio-based promos for Paul McCartney and Wings. Sheena McCoy, with whom I had made the Ferguson commercials, was soon back in my office with a script for Mandate, a men's aftershave featuring the popular French singer, Sasha Distel. We flew to a meeting with him at his home in Megève and the script was agreed leading to a production at Twickenham Studios. At the same time, I was preparing a Wings promo to be shot in the same studio and on one day had Sasha and Paul McCartney both having lunch in the nearby Italian restaurant.

Music of a rather different kind was involved when I was asked to produce a commercial for the launch of Jeff Wayne's *War of the Worlds*. We were to shoot at the London Planetarium and there was a lot of uncertainty about the exposure and how the images would turn out. In the event all was okay.

I was in the office one morning when the phone rang and it was Sheena asking if the director Mike Hodges and I could be available the following week for a shoot in Los Angeles.

After a quick check I was able to say yes, but what was the job and why the hurry? Sheena was by now a producer at J. Walter Thompson and the production was for Campari. The original very well-known commercial featuring Lorraine Chase had been produced by Garretts. And I suspect was possibly directed by Dick Clement. For whatever reason, his company Witzend, had been chosen to make this new commercial. This might explain why L.A. was chosen as the location.

Two weeks before the shoot date, the agency was told that Dick was not available for the shoot and the commercial would be directed by Ian La Frenais. This last-minute switching of directors had been a feature of Garretts in the past and had, by now, largely been overcome. It did not go down well then or on this occasion and the agency cancelled the job, hence the phone call.

Arriving in L.A. at about 2 pm local time, we met up with the already employed location manager who turned out to be of a considerable age. We went straight to look at his first recommendation. To say that it was a disaster is an understatement. There can't have been fewer patches of grass in the city that got less sunlight than this one. The sun actually reached the location for just over two hours in the day. Added to this, it was one block away from a freeway and there was an adjacent building site where I discovered they were due to start pouring concrete the day of our shoot. I found it hard to believe this was a serious option and confidence in our location manager was at an all time low.

Next morning we set out on a new search and were taken to one or two much better options, including a couple of great houses built by 19th century entrepreneurs. We finally settled on a more conventional, but still quite impressive, house where we were able to film the storyboard that showed a lady serving Campari drinks on a silver tray to her decorators. This was the second time I found myself in conflict with Witzend. It was going to be far from being the last.

I was to make one more Campari commercial on a much smaller scale with Sheena. It involved a man being concealed in a wardrobe only to be discovered by a returning husband. All was well when it was discovered that he was hiding with the new small bottles of ready-mixed Campari although quite why we were never told. It was not long after this that I was shooting a Babycham commercial at Luton Hoo, the one-time home of the

Wherner family and their fabulous collection of Fabergé eggs. The house, which is now a very superior hotel, has been used as a location for many feature films but we were only shooting a reception in the grounds for our client. During the morning, I received a phone call from my office to tell me that Sheena had been killed in a riding accident. Having brought up her son as a single mother in times when it must have been very difficult, she had by now married and was living near Cambridge. It was a sad day when my wife and I drove up to her funeral. She was a skilled producer and a great loss to J. Walter Thompson.

It was through our New York office that I was put in touch with a client from the Mobil Oil Company. The company, as part of their advertising strategy, sponsored programmes that were shown on the public broadcasting networks in the U.S., and they needed a presenter to introduce the programmes and add a summing up postscript. I put forward a young director and was asked to put in a bid. The bid was competitive and I was almost certainly bidding against Witzend. The client's chosen presenter was Peter Ustinov, an obvious choice as the initial project was to be filmed at Agatha Christie's home in Devon and, of course, Peter had played Hercule Poirot, one of her most enduring characters.

We had a minor problem trying to find a suitable date for the filming and to try to sort it out I organised a lunch with my client, the director and Peter's agent, Steve Kennis, who was the UK head of the William Morris Agency. My chosen venue for the lunch – remember, this was when lunches could last quite a long time – was the basement restaurant of the Tate Gallery on the Embankment.

Why the Tate? Because they had one of the best wine cellars in London and the wine list was so extensive that the menu was printed on the last page. The food was also pretty good and basically traditional English, just the place to take American clients where we would be surrounded by the murals painted by Whistler. As was my custom, I had arrived first at the table and checked that the white wine I had ordered was in the cooler and the claret had been decanted. I soon saw a gentleman being directed to my table and stood up as he arrived. "Steve Kennis?" I enquired and he took the seat opposite. The conversation went as follows. "What would you like to drink?" I said. "I don't drink at lunchtime," he replied. "So you don't know why we are meeting here?" "No, in fact, I said to my secretary why have I got to go to the goddam Tate?" "Well take a look at the wine list. I have an excellent Meursault on ice and a Chateau bottled claret has been decanted." He took the wine list and looked over it for some time before exclaiming, "This wine is on allocation in California, it is very difficult to find." "Well we had better try a bottle," I said and ordered one. He did drink that lunchtime and I discovered that his family was the Rothschild's importers in the U.S., so he really *did* know his wines. The meeting finally broke up with agreement on a date, having cancelled at least one appointment at about 4 pm.

On that shoot I thought that Peter Ustinov would also know his wines so sent the unit by train to check into our hotel, the Imperial in Torquay, while the client and I picked up Peter from his London apartment in a chauffeur-driven Daimler. We drove to Bristol where I had arranged lunch at Harveys of Bristol, the wine makers and home of Bristol Cream Sherry. After lunch we resumed our journey to Devon. The shoot, which was very straightforward, was to become one of several more I produced for that client. One was shot at the Old Vic Theatre where the production was Nicholas Nickelby, another with the author, John Mortimer, shot at his home. Peter did not really like having to wear a dinner jacket for every shoot and the dedication in one of his books that he gave me said of his photo on the cover, "Why am I smiling? Because I am not wearing a tuxedo."

There was one shoot that was not with Peter, rather with an ex-war correspondent, Eric Sevareid, an American war reporter and the location was to be the original, and still-preserved, war rooms under the Foreign Office in London. As usual it was a competitive bid and I did not take any crew more than I needed. At lunchtime, our caterers were parked in King Charles Street behind the Foreign Office and, having completed filming underground, we had a break before shooting again at about 4.30 pm.

During this break I was talking to the caterer when I was approached by a union representative wanting to know what was going on. I was technically undercrewed and working myself as assistant director, so he could have caused trouble. The salvation was that I was not making a commercial and he had no authority over me as I was working for America and not the UK.

When the unit reassembled, I questioned them about the incident, but they were all crew I regularly worked with and they were all shocked that such an obscure and secluded location should have come to the notice of the union. I realised later that the informant must have been Witzend, Dick Clement's company. The information had to have come from someone who had quoted on the job and knew the location and date.

I had been awarded the Campari contract originally placed with Witzend, beaten them to achieve the Chrysler contract and now held the Mobil business. They cannot have been too happy. This was not to be the last time I was to bid against Witzend and win!

Earlier I wrote about the commercial I had made at Pearl & Dean for an American men's fragrance called British Sterling. And I said there was something further to say about that commercial later. Fifteen years later, in 1980, I was in my office one afternoon when I took a call from Jim who was in our New York office. He asked me to look at a script that had been quoted on by one of my colleagues, the price was too high and we were going to loose the job. I got a copy of the script and was amazed to see that it was virtually the same script I had produced fifteen years earlier. The product was now with a new agency and the only difference in the script was that they had written in the Tower of London and Tower Bridge, which would have been much more difficult to achieve, if not impossible.

I immediately rang the agency and suggested that I could provide the Houses of Parliament at a much lower cost. I also sent an assistant to take Polaroids that I then sent to them via Concorde courier, which guaranteed delivery by noon the next day. A new estimate was accepted and this time we cast a very experienced horsewoman who just happened to be the wife of a champion jockey. We shot the commercial in beautiful early morning light some two weeks later.

The marketing director of the company, Speidel. had intended coming over for the shoot but had to cancel at the last minute. So it was a pleasant surprise when a few days later I received a phone call asking if I was the Geoff who had produced this great commercial. It was the marketing director who had been given my name by the agency and decided to call and thank me for the job. During the course of the conversation it transpired that he was planning a holiday in England and asked me if I knew a particular person in the industry whose house he might be renting. My wife and I were planning to take our three children to Disney World in Florida at almost the same time and I found myself saying, "Why not take our house?" By the end of the conversation it was all settled.

All I had to do now was tell my wife that I had invited a total stranger to use our house while we were away! I had arranged to meet our guests at Gatwick Airport and spend two days with them before we left for the States. As I stood in the crowd scanning the arrivals for a couple with two daughters, it suddenly dawned on me that I had no idea who I was looking for. Were they tall or short? Fat or thin? I hadn't a notion. Eventually they appeared well behind the rest of the passengers, the airline having lost half their baggage.

Our two families became great friends and remain so to this day.

In 1985, I was approached by the New York office of J. Walter Thompson to produce a Ford commercial for the American market featuring Jackie Stewart, who had a contract with the Ford Motor Company. We were to shoot in Glasgow with Jackie for the new Ford Mustang. Starting with a location at Glasgow Green and following this at the Museum of Transport where Jackie's 1971 Tyrell was on display. The following day was given over to various driving shots in and around Glasgow and finally we filmed a dialogue sequence with Jackie at the local college of education where they had a small studio.

The shoot was scheduled for 21 January, and for the following two days, I had no less than five agency representatives on the shoot. This was some indication of the importance of the commercial to the agency. It was the start of Jackie's contract which would result in my producing commercials with him over the next two or three years. The bid had, of course, been competitive but I had no idea who the opposition might be. (It was, of course, Witzend)

As it was winter, it came as no surprise to find our first location with a considerable covering of snow despite a general thaw and generally fine weather. The previous day, I had one of those incredible strokes of luck that make one think that someone is looking after you when, returning to the hotel, I found myself following a water jetting company van. I noted the phone number and the next morning they were on the location and washed away all signs of snow in the background of our scenes.

The next commercial with Jackie was to be filmed the following year at his house in Switzerland and the surrounding area. It was completed satisfactorily and without incident, but I did discover locally a low loader trailer that enabled filming while travelling without which had previously been a problem of the car looking unnaturally high on the road. The last commercial with Jackie that I was to quote on was to take place on location in Monaco and involved Jackie driving round the Corniche. I was fairly familiar with the area and the facilities available locally having worked in the area on more than one occasion. A great deal of helicopter filming was required and my director insisted on a camera operator who was very experienced in this specialised area. I knew that I could hire a local pilot and helicopter from Nice Airport and, having done my homework, knew that he had filmed car chases along the Corniche for Victorine Studios Nice and knew the area well. My director said that the operator would not fly with anyone other than a particular pilot but I stood my ground. It was, after all, another competitive bid.

Before the bid had been completed, I received a phone call in my office from the pilot in question who seemed to have cornered the UK market for helicopter work and clearly thought he was God's gift to advertising suggesting as he did that I would need his services. To say I was furious is an understatement, not only because he knew I was preparing an estimate but with his arrogance and assumption that he knew better than me how to do my job. Why would I want to employ a UK pilot, pay him an inflated salary, hotel and living expenses for a minimum of three days, and hire a helicopter when I had a more locally experienced pilot available virtually on an hourly basis. It was as they say a no brain decision and of course we won the day and our camera operator did not refuse to fly with our local pilot

All of our shoots with Jackie were produced for the agency in New York by a young producer who usually had two senior agency creatives with him. As I often did on location shoots, I arranged a dinner for the agency and I had read an article about a Swiss chef who had opened a new restaurant in Monaco. Unusually, I had my wife with me on location as she had just come out of hospital following an operation for cancer and I had been refused time off by Jim Garrett. We booked a table for eight for dinner at the new restaurant. We had a memorable meal with aubergine flowers prepared in cream between starters and the main course. I was a little embarrassed when our young producer asked for "A tomato and onion salad, and a well-done steak." This was likely the first time the chef had to prepare such a request. The agency decided to return the compliment and invited us to their hotel, Loews, for a hamburger.

I had already made a Timex commercial when I was able to use the "Red Berets" or Paras, supplemented with actors from the film *A Bridge Too Far*. I was to produce another Timex commercial, this time for their New York agency and it was also to throw up several challenges.

I suspect that the script was the result of the popularity at the time of hovercraft, as it called for one to be seen travelling across a snow-covered landscape. I found myself working with a director from another company, but I cannot remember how that came about. We looked at more than one possible location in Switzerland and eventually settled on the Jungfrau Glacier. There is a hotel at Kleine Scheidegg, roughly half way up the mountain railway that ran from Grindelwald to the end of the line at the top of the glacier. This was to be our unit hotel before travelling by train each morning up to the glacier. We had a small hovercraft and brought it out from the UK lifting it by helicopter to our chosen spot on the glacier. There were arguments with the agency over the cost but they were easily justified. The client, however, demanded the return of the vehicle after the shoot.

The client also told us that the craft would not work at the altitude at which we were filming. I argued that all we needed was a couple of seconds of actual travelling and chose to ignore the problem. So well so good, as they say, but I suddenly got a radio message from the unit which was several kilometres away from our base in the Jungfrau café to say that our driver had run the hovercraft into a small crevasse and they needed the helicopter to help retrieve it. That was not a problem as it was sitting outside our base, but the agency creative director was at that moment boarding it to visit the location and I was in the unfortunate position of having to stop him. All was duly sorted out and the hovercraft completed its assignment as planned, even if it was being towed by our helicopter.

At the end of the shoot, the helicopter had to lift the hovercraft over the mountain pass and lower it to the nearest point where it could be transported by road. At dinner that evening, we got a call to say that the helicopter had encountered a strong wind over the pass and had jettisoned its load. So much for the client wanting his expensive vehicle returned. It was left on the mountain before it was eventually collected and scrapped. A good job it was not hired.

I have been fortunate in working on several series of commercials and I went to New York representing a young director new to the company. He had a showreel that included several dialogue commercials and this seemed to impress the agency I was going to see about an American Express contract. We won the job and it was the start of several shoots often with personalities of some importance that was, after all, the point of the campaign which ended with the line, "Don't leave home without it".

My first shoot was for two commercials, one in Rome with an American doctor, Tenley Albright, who had been an Olympic figure skating champion followed by a move to Switzerland and filming with Jean-Claude Killy, an Olympic downhill skiing champion and now a respected member of the Swiss Olympic Committee. The first shoot in Rome went well despite our star insisting on rollerskating in the reception of our rather smart hotel. It was then down to me to send some unit members back to the UK and take others with me to Megève in Switzerland. We had some quite sophisticated equipment with us and I had something like three thousand pounds worth of excess baggage. I had a considerable delay in negotiating the payment and the crew, agency and client (rather unusually we had an American Express client with us), went ahead with my personal luggage. By the time I was free to depart, I had to run to the departure gate. As luck would have it, I reached it just in time to see the plane leaving.

There was no other flight to Geneva that evening and the only way of getting to our Swiss location was to fly via Zurich. But I could only get a seat by upgrading to first class. When I had talked about our transfer to Megève with my agency producer, I had said that we would be going via the Gotthard Tunnel which was to become rather relevant as it turned out. I eventually arrived at Geneva Airport and went straight to the Avis desk where I had pre-booked two 7-seater cars. "Had the unit taken snow chains with the other car?" I asked the receptionist. "No," she answered. So I took two sets and headed off to find the unit and our hotel. My journey was not easy, I was very tired and was given a very small scale map which I could hardly see leading to my finding myself on the wrong side a mountain and having to retrace my steps. Eventually I found my way to the hotel, and asking in my best French if the unit had arrived with my luggage, I discovered that they had not arrived.

There followed an anxious evening with no dinner as it was the start of the season and the hotel had opened especially for us and it was far too late to find food elsewhere. The next day the unit and client arrived having had to book into another hotel for the night at some distance. The producer had remembered my saying that we would go through the Gotthard Tunnel. But when he got there it had been closed due to heavy snowfalls. Red faces all round but all was well in the end. Other commercials were to follow, with the originator of the Muppets, Jim Henson, Count Basie and the Duke of Bedford. I met with the Duke for tea in Claridge's. He was not allowed to return to Woburn Abbey having left it to live in France. So when it came to a location for his commercial, I hired Hever Castle in Kent.

I remember saying the Americans will not know the difference! Being fond of the occasional glass of wine, I was very sorry that a shoot in the Rothschild's wine cellar in France was cancelled at short notice, I believe through illness.

The client really wanted a member of the Royal family but this was not, of course, possible. I knew the details of the fees payable for a thirty-second commercial and the additional sum for a fifteen-second cut down. At a meeting in New York I remembered having seen a TV documentary on the last remaining private army in Europe. Not recalling the exact details, a little research revealed that it had been the Atholl Highlanders, the private force belonging to the Duke of Atholl. Although not actively employed since Victoria's time, it still existed and trooped the colour outside the Duke's home at Blair Atholl Castle each year.

I was asked to follow up and see if I could set up a deal with the Duke. I returned to London and arranged a meeting with the Duke at the House of Lords. A deal was agreed to film with him at the annual trooping of the colour ceremony. It was something that I looked forward to.

In my office one afternoon I took a phone call from America to tell me that the client had cancelled the project. The reason given was, "he could not put on American television a man with a name like Atholl." Think about it!

Maureen Lipman's memorable performances in the series of BT commercials will live in the memory for years to come. I was fortunate to win the contract for the first series from the agency J. Walter Thompson but there were to be all sorts of problems along the way. My director was Richard Loncraine and the agency writer, Richard Phillips, were destined never to get on, but we should go back to the beginning. The casting of Maureen was the subject of much discussion and considerable opposition. The main bone of contention was her age and how could she portray a grandmother. Did any of you question it? My personal view was and is that she was a superb actress and more than capable of playing an older person.

Look at *Dad's Army* that we still see on TV regularly. The bumbling Sgt. Jones played by the actor Clive Dunn was aged forty-two when the series started.

There was further disagreement when an account executive tried to veto the casting of a black newsagent with some very racist remarks. He was put in his place and the actor got the job. Richard Loncraine was shooting when it came time to do a screen test with Maureen and I found myself in the director's chair. She performed a brilliant monologue although I felt she should never have been asked. The next and more serious problem was that Richard Phillips wanted to shoot more commercials than I believe the client had agreed to do. So there was some difficulty with the budget trying to accommodate his demands. A further problem was that he had not written final scripts to a given length, preferring to see how they played out. This was to lead to serious conflict with my director, and worse, it upset Maureen. By constantly asking for changes, or extra takes, I suspect that Maureen felt that her performance was being questioned and she became visibly distressed. By lunchtime the inevitable happened and Richard Loncraine refused to come back on set after the break.

I was put in the unenviable position of having a crew basically loyal to Loncraine and I had to try to keep the shoot going until I could resolve the problem in some way. We did continue filming the "Ology" sequence and I managed to get agreement from the agency to bring in a new director the next day. The new director was Tony Smith, who had a very good record with recent success on television. The rest, as they say, is history. Communication, whether in sound or vision, is what advertising is all about. What you see on the screen is very often what the director or client wants you to see. On many occasions a sequence of shots will convince you that the next shot is part of the same sequence when it might have been shot at a different time in a different location or even in a different country.

I have already mentioned a shampoo commercial where I had to reproduce a pack shot in a small studio to appear as though it had been shot in Venice, but there were many other occasions where clever technique could and did fool the audience. When the pack shot of a cigarette commercial shot in South Africa proved unsatisfactory, I hired a small studio in Soho and with the aid of a piece of plain carpet, some dried grasses and pampas grass from the local florist, nobody knew that it had not been shot in the original wide open spaces of the original location.

There was to be a much more dramatic example when I was asked to produce a commercial for Gilbey's gin. The script was brilliant bearing in mind that the spot was for transmission in several European countries. It featured the well-known actor, Terry Thomas, known to a generation of filmgoers as the quintessential English cad. He was to be seen trying to impress a young lady over a glass of Gilbey's in a language best described as franglais, a meaningless mixture of English, French, German, Spanish and Italian. At the end of his attempt to convince his young companion, he raises his glass and asks her, "Care for an autre?", and we cut to a black screen with the Union Jack and the caption, "Drink Gilbey's and you'll understand the English". It was a very clever way of covering several countries at a very reasonable cost.

Unfortunately, the client did not like our choice of companion for Terry and we were called upon to recast and shoot new scenes to be intercut. My agency producer Ray knew a young actress who he thought was right for the part and in a small Soho studio we shot a new set of reverse angles (Terry's POV). The young actress was Rula Lenska, and the resulting commercial was a great success.

Back to my position as a director of James Garrett and Partners. I had been asked to sign papers as a director of a New York company which I knew nothing about and was asked to assign a contract for a commercial I was producing to a company in Liechtenstein, again a company I had no knowledge of. As with my splitting with Kenneth Hume, I was not happy at being put into a situation that was, at the very least, of doubtful legality. Added to this I was occasionally paid in cash, a wad of fifty pound notes that I was warned not to pay into the bank! This was to lead to a decision to resign from the board and threaten to become freelance.

Jim's reaction? An immediate doubling of my salary, which says a lot about my value to the company!!

I continued to be offered other jobs and was on more than one occasion offered a salary of £100,000 a year. However, there was always a catch with any company making such an outrageous offer. They would be expecting me to contribute the two or three million in turnover that I was contributing to Garretts. A creative business does not work like that, even the best producer is dependent upon the popularity, or otherwise, of his director to, at least, some extent.

Approaches from production companies could not be thwarted by Jim, not so approaches from agencies. Jim had a well-established network of informants based largely on entertaining lavishly and, not infrequently, giving employment to an executive's mistress. This network, together with the fact that all mail was opened and read by Jim, ensured that he was always one jump ahead of any proposed move and could always put a spanner in the works.

Despite my continuing relationship with Procter & Gamble, they were fully aware that I would not stop working on their competitors' brands. But even so, to produce a major relaunch for Persil was directly in conflict with some of my P&G work. The commercial was to be a musical extravaganza featuring a young presenter supported by a group of dancers and a group of actors representing all the major washing machine manufacturers with the refrain, "And so say all of us," in response to the presenter's claim saying how good the product was.

We shot the commercial on a large stage in Shepperton Studios and used every bit of space, so much so that the camera was actually outside the stage for the final wide shot. It was the first time I had a cameraman use a searchlight for a set taking up the full width and height of the stage. Who was our choreographer? None other than Bruno Tonioli.

I mentioned earlier that I had found Cliff Owen to be, to say the least, insensitive to his actors. I continued to work with him at Garretts, but fell out on two or three more occasions when he became what I can only call bloody-minded. As a feature director, Cliff had directed one film with Peter Sellers, but was possibly not considered for another. On commercials he would not shoot out of sequence whatever the cost and would always include every shot in the first cut. On more than one occasion, I found myself sitting with a creative director re-editing the cut.

There were two occasions when a budget was seriously affected by Cliff's attitude. Once on a large stage at Pinewood Studios we were shooting a drinks commercial, (I think it was for a major brand of Port) when, without warning, Cliff said he wanted to start on a photo of the subject actor. This had never been discussed and the whole crew had to sit around until one could be found and delivered to the studio. The second occasion was much more serious and the subject was a commercial for Kleenex tissues. The script called for a bus full of people who all sneezed in unison, causing the bus to jump as a result. Cliff said that he would need the bus to be rigged with a crane following it to lift it off the ground. Clearly this would have been out of question with the client's budget.

It was time for me to overrule my director so I hired a bus and one or two extras and took it down to the back lot at Shepperton. The simple laying of a piece of timber that was probably not more than three by two inches for the bus to drive over produced a very acceptable bounce and we won the job.   The shoot took place and should have been very simple and straightforward, but Cliff decided otherwise and was determined to have his own way. He turned it into a full day and insisted on keeping a bus full of extras until they were on overtime rates completely unnecessarily.

On one more shoot at a pub somewhere in North London, I was not happy with the progress we were making and made it clear. I was sharply told, "If you want to direct it, then fucking well do it." Maybe I should have done!

I was to make many commercials for cars. From the launch of the Ford Transit to the launch many years later of the Ford Fiesta, several American Fords with Jackie Stewart, the launch of the Avenger and the Chrysler Sunbeam, along with spots for BMW, Austin and Peugeot.

Most were fairly straightforward, but one or two are deserving of mention. The first was a Talbot shoot where the script called for a car to be dropped from an aircraft with the presenter coming down a using parachute. I soon became aware of every aircraft that could fit the bill and we eventually agreed on a particular aircraft that was frequently used to transport horses for a well-known Irish racehorse owner.

I agreed to use a Royal Air Force loading team and spent a long time trying to arrange insurance. Our location was to be Duxford, the home of the aircraft museum, but still an RAF station. I had very specific requirements because to lower the presenter I would need a 200 ft. hydraulic platform and a crane capable of lifting cars into place on an enormous T for Talbot logo made from white gravel laid out on a grass area. Both of these vehicles weighed about forty tons and had very wide turning circles so the approach had to be capable of taking the weight. On the recce we found a suitable area, but my director saw a small building in the background and insisted that it had to be removed. I simply had to point out that if it was in shot, he was certainly not shooting the storyboard.

The shoot started well but before long the hydraulic tower cables got tangled and it became useless. Then the weather closed in and, naturally enough, the aircraft failed to arrive. At this point I must make another comment on the vital importance of the quote letter. If working on an outside location that could be affected by weather, you have to include a weather day figure. On this commercial the figure had to include all the heavy equipment that was in the original estimate. So it was a very high figure that was to stand us in good stead as we shall see. Without the plane, I hired a helicopter from which we eventually dropped our feature car so that, at least, we had it falling through the air. It was also used for a shot of the presenter (or a stand in) descending by parachute. On his first jump, the wind caught him and he landed on the wing of the Concorde parked in the museum area. All eventually went well but we did need another day, but were well covered. When the commercial was edited and presented to the client he was not happy with the result. Although I had worked on Talbot commercials many times when the account was with Grant Advertising, the brand had been taken over by the French Peugeot company and the client had promised his new management that they would get a commercial showing the car being ejected from a plane, not dropping from a helicopter.

It was time for a little more film trickery and I set about trying to satisfy a disappointed client. I was incredibly lucky to find a suitable cargo plane on the ground at Manston Airport in Kent, and I hired it for a day. With the aid of my RAF loading team, a large wind machine and the camera moving past the static plane as the car was pushed out of it, this was another example of deceiving the eye of the viewer. The commercial was re-edited and satisfied the client, but both versions were tested on a captive audience and the helicopter version was eventually transmitted. It was a great success and exceeded all sales expectations.

"Diamonds are a girls best friend", or so the song goes, and we set out to prove it with a commercial for De Beers, the famous diamond merchants. The script called for a young lady to be seen waiting on a snow-clad station platform for her partner to arrive. I had at the time a regular driver in the South of France and I called him up to drive me and the two women who were the creative group on the account on a recce to find a location that would fit the bill. We spent some four days travelling around France and eventually settled on a mountain route some twenty miles outside Grenoble. There was a station at some distance from a small village with a hotel opposite across a gravel square. Yet again I was working with a French director who was insisting on bringing catering from Paris, something I refused to accept. In fact, the small country hotel provided some of the best catering I have ever experienced.

I had carefully researched the likelihood of snow and from all the records we should have had two snowfalls by the time of the shoot. All we got was drizzle but it was enough to trigger our weather day insurance. I had managed to hire a main line train from SNCF for one day but we eventually kept it for three. I am not quite sure how! Snow was, of course, the problem. There was a tunnel entrance just outside the station, so we needed to have the hillside covered in snow. Today one could simply hire a snow machine, but no such thing existed in those days so it was a mixture of a spray usually used to dull or eliminate difficult highlights to cover the mirror in which our heroine was to see herself and, I am ashamed to say in retrospect, detergent foam. By the end of the shoot, we had bought every available drum of detergent between our location and the Swiss border. We had also hired the local fire brigade who had to spray the foam on the rails and the hillside over the tunnel. Our young suitor was to present the lady with a £5,000 diamond necklace as he alighted from the train. I had carried it from London in a money belt and it was kept securely in the hotel safe when not needed. It was to take some time for our fire brigade to achieve an acceptable snow scene over the tunnel entrance and meanwhile our actor was trapped in the train with the engine running and no ventilation. We had all overlooked a potentially very serious situation. Fortunately, he survived and met his sweetheart with the necklace.

Another commercial I was to produce in France was for Coca Cola. I had to fly to New York to attend a briefing meeting with two other production companies, my competitors. This was a totally new experience. I was to quote on two different scripts, one calling for a location abroad and one to be shot in the UK involving a firework display for which I had the perfect location in mind.

Apart from being a competitive bid, the production was to be on a cost plus basis, in other words all costs had to be justified or money refunded, something Jim Garrett would not be happy with. I undertook a reece with the agency producer and on our tour of possible locations based on the area around Nice we came across a small hotel in the village of Roquefort-les-Pins and had a memorable lunch. It may have been irrelevant to the commercial but was to become a favourite, for my wife and me. As a result of the trip, I had two possible locations. We needed a bar as a base and with incredible luck found one in a village that today is a massive tourist attraction. The owner of what in those days was the main bar/restaurant, was going to close for a week as he took a holiday and he agreed to us taking over his bar as our location. It seems incredible today that such a deal could be done but things were very different in the 1980s.

We had an alternative location on the coast in the village of Villefranche, but the two possible sites had different requirements. The coastal location would give us greater logistical problems and mean paying fees to adjoining buildings, while the inland location needed more expense in other areas. I had to budget to cover either as it was not to be my decision. Once the decision was made, we set about casting a group of youths capable of downing a glass or can of Coca Cola in one gulp...not easy. The casting sessions took place at Victorine Studios in Nice and the inland location was selected. We had a very successful shoot and it became memorable for the lunches in the village hostelry that overlooked the square that was our set. I was to make several productions in France with different directors, both English and French. But I usually had invaluable help from a French production manager, Caroline Mazauric, and she became an important part of any unit, English or French.

I was asked to produce a commercial for Bacardi Rum with an American director and the chosen location was to be Antigua. I was fortunate in being able to book my whole unit on a package holiday deal that kept the budget down but proved not to have been ideal as the holiday company went broke during our stay. Fortunately it did not seem to impact our schedule, and we were duly returned to the UK as arranged. The agency was JWT in London and was based on the fact that Bacardi could be used with various mixers, the title was "Bacardi Shorts". There were also stills to be taken on the location and we took a wardrobe mistress with us to supervise both stills and film. My director decided that he wanted to start with a close-up of a flower embroidered on the back of a pair of shorts worn by our young female lead. The wardrobe mistress was called upon but could not provide a satisfactory result. Calling on my grandmother's embroidery lessons, I took over and it was my effort that won the day.

The next demand from the director was that our young couple should be seen in the local market searching for fruit while carrying a block of ice in a string bag that was fashionable at the time. Directors can often cause problems for producers by making unexpected requests but when you are on a remote location they can provide a very real challenge. I tried everywhere to locate a block of ice even approaching a naval ship in English Harbour with no success. There was nothing for it but to produce one ourselves. After a visit to a local store, I came back with a saw, some wood, and a plastic tablecloth. Whereupon I was able to make a small box lined with the tablecloth, fill it with water and place it in the hotel deep freeze. A block of ice was duly produced, but what to carry it in? Yes, I had to find a string bag. It had to be string so that the ice could be seen (and drip). Having once on a camping holiday won a treasure hunt by producing ten rows of knitting using a ball of string and two pencils, I saw no difficulty in creating an acceptable bag which I duly did sitting outside my hotel room with string stretched between two beach chairs. Apart from the unit and agency team, nobody ever knew who did what on a very challenging location.

One major advantage that comes with experience is the ability to judge a production manager or assistant producer as to their knowledge and reliability, often in just one conversation.

I have already mentioned Caroline, my French contact, but there were several others including, Goffredo Matassi, an excellent production manager who worked for me in Italy. I also had good contacts in New Zealand, America, Spain, and South Africa. I owe each and every one of them a huge debt of gratitude for their hard work for which I usually received the credit.

The producers were put on a bonus scheme in the late eighties and bonuses were paid if you came in under budget. I suspect this was a double-edged weapon that could work to Jim's advantage when budgets were exceeded. I took on the largest project the company had ever undertaken and this could have been my downfall.

The agency creative team was assigned to another producer, but I was friendly with the art director who lived in Sussex and travelled in with me from Haywards Heath. Jim was not at all happy that I was trying to take over a project that he thought should have gone to someone else, but with a budget well in excess of a million pounds, and a very demanding schedule, I was supported by another company director who believed that I was the only producer who could successfully handle the project. In the event, I completed the project under budget and turned in a £400,000 profit for the company. Shortly after my return to the UK from the location in America, Jim decided to take a holiday despite being paranoid about others doing so. As he left I was handed a memo, not by Jim (but by Mike Gilmour as Jim had already left), which informed me that he had for some time been considering changing the producer's bonus system, thereby reducing the amounts paid. My bonus for the American shoot was several thousand pounds, and he wanted to back date the changes to cover and so reduce this amount. I was, naturally enough, furious. And on his return I confronted him and accused him of double standards and breaking the terms of my contract.

He had no leg to stand on and duly apologised and paid me the full bonus. But he cannot have been happy.

The project that was for Esso, or as it was known in the U.S., Exxon, was a return to an old theme based on a cartoon character. It had a jingle with the line "The Esso sign means happy motoring". But this was to be no cartoon. Far from it. The idea was that cars were to be seen in a fairground setting, with cars on a big dipper, a roundabout and a Helter Skelter. The problem was that the commercial was destined for the UK, and I was faced with the problem of locating cars in or near L.A. that would be acceptable in the British market. The director, yet again, was Richard Loncraine, who had a fear of flying and decided that he would travel by sea and then drive across to our location on the West Coast. I made arrangements for the hire of a large Winnebago and he duly travelled to the location with his personal assistant. I had been introduced by our local representative to a locally-based producer who would work with me. The producer also brought in his wife who was an excellent production accountant. Her enormous contribution was that she kept the production accounts up to date on a daily basis, and so efficiently that on completion her accounts were entered into the company's books without comment.

I flew to L.A. to attend budget meetings with the relevant local crew, construction manager, and special effects supervisor and a budget was eventually agreed. Within days of my return to London new figures were coming in showing that we were heading for a serious overspend.

This was serious and I was told to get back out there and sort it out. I flew back on 14 August, 1990, my elder daughter's thirtieth birthday. I needed to bang heads together and come up with some really creative ideas. A week later I was on my way back to London having stayed up all night on the flight and set out my ideas in a lengthy report.

Our chosen location was a dry lake bed in the Mojave Desert and it can best be described in an article from the Baker Valley News, Baker being the nearest, if at some distance, town.

I quote, *"Twenty miles north of Baker on State Route 127 is a normally dry lake. Silurian Lake sits in the middle of absolutely nowhere. It is flat, dry, empty, lonesome and utterly desolate. This is not a terribly attractive place to be. Comes now the good folks from Hollywood who are going to film a commercial for Esso Fuels, a Standard Oil brand sold in England and Europe."*

The article goes on to talk about the problems our construction manager was having with the wind and the forecast of storms to come. I should also mention that we had a team of stunt drivers who would be seen driving real cars as though they were fairground bumper cars in a giant cage while a tiger, yes a tiger, wandered around the outside of the cage.

There were so many different areas that had to be co-ordinated that the only way I had been able to get the costs under control was by carefully scheduling every item and effectively dictating the shooting schedule day by day. I was, yet again, doing the director's job. I had to schedule construction, a special effects team that would be responsible for keeping the cars going up and down on the carousel, our stunt drivers, a helicopter, several existing fairground rides for background and, not least, our tiger. The tiger was in Canada and was brought across the border, probably quite illegally, but that was the least of my worries.

Perhaps the best way of illustrating the problems I was faced with is to copy some of the report that I wrote on the flight back to London.

Summary of pre-production situation as at 21 August.

During the week commencing 13 August, when costings for various aspects of construction and effects work started to come in, it was apparent that the budget was being substantially exceeded and needed drastic surgery, if possible.

On my arrival it was evident that the information we had was not the whole picture as many set drawings had yet to be completed and therefore could not be costed with any accuracy. The first thing to be done was to examine what could be cut from the sets without running the risk of being seen to short change the client. The answer was effectively nothing, but there was scope for combining things and making the best use of the pieces we were building and stop further cost escalation.

Over the next two days the Roller Coaster was combined with a section of the Helter Skelter so that only one structure carrying a car at a height of twenty-five feet was required. The size of the cage was reduced and the number of bars cheated and made moveable for close-ups.

I suggested that rather than paying $22,000 to strike the set and transport it back to L.A., it could be sold on site for scrap. There were other obvious savings, the helicopter need not be on site and could remain at its base cutting out the need for a fuel bowser. There were three main suppliers contributing to the construction, the supply of the suitable vehicles and the operating of *the various effects and by scheduling every aspect of the production down to the absolute minimum time on location and not having any individual or piece of equipment on site for an hour longer than necessary I was able to identify the best part of $100,000 provided everything went according to plan!*

In the end it all worked out but the assistant director who would normally have expected to make a contribution by suggesting improvements to the schedule was taken aback when faced with my daily schedule and simply said, "I can't make any changes, can I?" "No," was my reply, every item was on the tightest possible schedule and nobody called for a day longer than needed.

On our penultimate day, the storm arrived and our set was basically torn apart and previously set up lights would have to be left to dry out. Please note that this represented the one and only occasion this particular producer had to concede defeat to the vagaries of the weather. Undaunted, I made the decision to wait until midday at which time, despite protests from Richard and the assistant director, I called a halt and shut down the production. We still needed at least one set up as we had to retake previously shot footage of our big dipper with rather more light. I knew that with what we had in the can, I could complete the storyboard with the aid of special effects. By cancelling the shoot, I was saving a substantial sum on crew salaries and other expenses. I had to stay on after the shoot to settle all the outstanding bills and sort out insurance claims where appropriate. I was also to negotiate a sale of the several constructions for scrap.

What An Engaging Couple. Geoff poses with Shirley Hammerton on the announcement of their engagement, 25 April, 1954.

A Night On The Town. Geoff with wife, Shirley, and director, Frank Worth.

And The Winner Is... The author anxiously awaits the judges' decision at the Television Mail Awards, 1967.

In Good Company. The late 1960s saw Geoff form a new company, Group 31, to provide office services to independent directors and producers.

Never Far From The Phone. On location in Los Angeles,
Geoff sports his favourite Snoopy jumper while enjoying
a small libation.

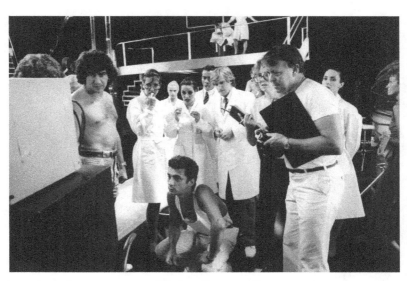

Dancing The Day Away. The author on the set of an all-singing,
all-dancing extravaganza for Persil at Shepperton Studios. To
Geoff's right is Italian choreographer, Bruno Tonioli.

Smile, Peter. You're Not Wearing A Tuxedo, Now. Sir Peter
became notoriously grumpy any time he was asked to
don a tuxedo. Here he is with Geoff and James Clavell at
a book launch – without one.

That's Not The Right Chair, Is It? Geoff listens intently as
Ronnie Corbett, sitting in a most unfamiliar chair,
enthralls crewmembers.

RONNIE CORBETT

2.1.79.

Dear Geoffrey,

It was very kind of you to take
the trouble to drop me a little note with my
clothes, there was no need to have worried
about the car at all in the event, because the
station I forgot was quite near the Theatre.
So all went perfectly smoothly and I got to
the Show with plenty of time to spare, but
thank you for your trouble and note.

Hope to see you soon, best wishes
for 1979.

Yours,

A Big Thank You From Him. A short note from a big star.
A treasured personal thank-you note from Ronnie
Corbett to the author.

A SOUPER NIGHT at Geoff Forster's

eoff Forster braved the rain to ignite a remarkable display of fireworks. General verdict was lat the rain made no difference to what was definitely the party of the year - so far.

Nancy Egerton samples the Cinefood

Sean Gilroy and Bob Tree of Osborne-Peacock mourning the passing of cigarette commercials with Vicky Sanders, of Doyle Dane Bernbach

Frank Evans, the well known film caterer, or conspirator, and wench

The Heinz 'Souperday' team (l to r): Geoff Forster, Nona Johnston, Johnny Johnston, Mrs Terry Taylor, Dennis Auton, Frank Worth, Ron Wyatt, Mrs Worth and Terry Taylor

Paul Woolston-Smith (left) at 10 pm and (right) at 2 am. Steve Wheeler was heard to s that he doesn't need a wig...

A few of the 180-plus people at the party watch the fireworks. If statistics interest you, between them they pol-ished off 60 bottles of spirits and vermouths, eight gallons of beer, 20 bottles of wine and 400 assorted minerals

(l to R): Frank Worth, Nona Johnston, Dominic Roncoroni and lady, and Mrs Wainman

Party Time. Geoff warmly welcomed 150 brave souls to his home in Chislehurst on a cold, wet November evening, where they were treated to a forty-foot mobile canteen, and more booze than you could shake a stick at, 1967.

265

Nobody has told anyone at GFA that selling is vulgar ... so the commercials they are briefed to make tend to set the cash registers ringing in the client's market place.

For the Associates, making commercials is a crafty art—a commercial art. They strive to translate the marketing platform intelligently—to shoot it creatively—produce it meticulously.

Concentration on detail adds up to a professional production technique with a healthy respect for schedules, delivery dates and realistic budgets ... and it's not just the big names either which make up the total—there's a wealth of behind-the-scenes talent in that bottom drawer.

Meet them at 31 Curzon Street, W.1. Talk with them ... judge for yourself.

DIAL 01-629 8681 SPEAK TO GEOFFREY FORSTER

Geoffrey Forster's Associates cause things to happen in the Till

Shameless Promotion. A trade press ad for Geoffrey Forster Associates in an effort to drum up more business. Cha-ching!

266

Flying Scotsman. Scottish racing car legend, Jackie Stewart, on the set of a Ford commercial at his home in Switzerland. This spot was one of many Geoff produced with Sir Jackie for J. Walter Thompson, New York.

That Bloody Phone Never Stops Ringing. Yet another shot of the author on the phone, this time in his office in London.

What Could Possibly Go Wrong? The finished set in the Mojave
Desert for an Esso commercial with Geoff as producer, 1990.

Hammering Out The Details. Geoff takes the Esso set construction into his own hands.

Everything Is Coming Together. An aerial view of the Mojave
Desert set for the Esso shoot.

Tiger By The Tail. One of the stars of the Esso commercial.
All will be purr-fectly fine.

Stormy Weather. The Esso set was basically destroyed
by high winds and rain.

I Can't Bear To Look. Another view of the devastation – probably
the only time the weather ever got the better of Geoff.

It had been a huge challenge but we had brought it off, but there was a sting in the tail. Within days of our return the first Gulf War broke out and most of our work proved in vain. Esso could hardly celebrate in the circumstances.

Throughout my career I have had many instances of coincidence or luck but nothing to compare with what happened at the client pre-production meeting. The director is usually in charge, or at least takes an active part in explaining how he is going to fulfill the brief, but Richard was already on his way and it fell to me. With a colleague, I waited for the client to enter the agency conference room and when he did he greeted me by name having worked with me before and he knew me well. It was the best possible start.

One of the achievements that I am proudest of was the re-establishing of a relationship that had not existed for many years. In the early days of commercial television, the company had been the major supplier to one of the premier advertising agencies, J. Walter Thompson. It had long since lost that position. A very good friend and client of mine (Mike) was eventually to become their head of television and we had agreed to have lunch when I joined Garretts, as I have already recounted.

During Mike's time as head of television at JWT, I began to produce more and more commercials for the agency and worked across the board regardless of the company rules. In fact, Mike did not want to have any other producer from the company handling their work.

The result was a steadily building turnover including some high profile projects such as British Telecom. We built the company turnover with JWT back to being the major supplier and held the position for not one but three years. It must have been a bitter pill for Jim to swallow and I was told to lay off other people's contacts in the agency. Shortly afterwards he offered Mike the job of Managing Director of James Garrett and Partners.

He was given no real power and it was a great pleasure to me after I had left to be able to introduce him to his next employment with an American consultancy with many blue chip international clients. They had tried to attract me, but I was not interested in starting up another company in London.

There are so many projects that I could talk about, but enough is enough.

When I started my commercial career having been employed as a trainee writer, my first script to be produced was for Lux soap, so perhaps I may be permitted to close this part of my history by returning to that product and two Lux projects that I was to produce. The first and most dramatic was with the German actress, Nastassja Kinski. Lux had for many years advertised with well-known and glamorous actresses and they would often have the choice of key technicians, probably the cameraman and almost certainly makeup and hairdresser. They could also have an influence on the choice of directors. On this particular project, the originally chosen location was in North Africa. That was until Nastassja said she would not shoot there. Quickly we rearranged the shoot for Spain. We were also advised that if she was going to be accompanied by her husband and child, we could have problems.

The choice of director was a photographer who had worked with her in the past, Eva Sereny, who had recently won a BAFTA award with a short film, *The Red Dress*. She was agreed with Nastassja, and so we set about wardrobe preparation with a well-known French stylist. A fitting was set up for London where our star was staying at the Savoy. There were delays and nerves were becoming a little taut. I had provided a car with a mobile phone to take Nastassja and her family to London Airport for their flight to Malaga. I had made reservations for the family at the Marbella Club and booked a dinner for all the key players in anticipation of her arrival.

The fact that I knew more about her whereabouts than the agency producer was to cause some irritation but it was my job to know whether or not our star was going to turn up. She did turn up, complete with husband, baby and nanny. Though she did disappear to her room on arrival and then put in a very brief appearance at the dinner. She had her choice of cameraman, makeup artiste, and hairdresser and there followed a day of testing and agreeing the styling and wardrobe. The choice of cameraman, who was Italian, caused a problem as he refused to work with any light that had been used before and demanded a completely new set of bulbs. Apparently there was often no love lost between the Italians and the

Spanish who, of course, were my electricians. With a Dutch location manager, a Canadian agency producer and others from the UK and several northern European countries, I had more than a dozen nationalities on the crew.

My cameraman did not satisfy himself with only being bloody-minded about the lights, he refused to shoot when we had a perfect set up because our generator had not yet arrived on the location, despite the fact that it was not needed. He also told Nastassja that he could not photograph her through the autocue glass that we had provided because she had to deliver dialogue in different languages. All of these problems or irritations, which is what they really were, were still to come but after our dinner together when Nastassja had arrived, my director, Eva, was clearly suffering a crisis of confidence. It was serious and at three o'clock in the morning I was sitting on the end of her bed trying to talk sense into her and bolster her confidence. In the end, all was well and after a difficult start, we had a very successful shoot.

My last film for Lux was with the Italian star Ornella Muti, and it was to be directed by perhaps the best director that I ever had the pleasure of working with, the feature director Karel Reisz, director of *The French Lieutenant's Woman,* among other high profile films. We had a good shoot in Rome, notable only for the fact that I had a severe back problem after filming at dawn outside the Trevi Fountain in December, and the fact that the Italian banks went on strike.

Eventually my production manager was to arrange for me to go to the bank under guard and enter by another building so that I could withdraw the funds I had deposited – some £30,000. It was illegal, of course, according to Italian law at the time, but I had financed the production by putting £10,000 on each of my three credit cards, Visa, Amex and Diners. No wonder the bank manager took me to the bankers' dinner in Eastbourne! Having got the cash from the bank my problems started. No credit card bills could be paid in Italy so I had to try and find a way to get the cash back to the UK. There followed three days of negotiation and failure, instructions to contact a certain official at the bank resulted in another refusal. The problem was that the cash had been deposited in an exterior account and could not be transferred back to the UK.

Eventually we found that there were two possible ways to transfer the cash, to take it to the Vatican and have them post it back or to transfer it through the Mafia which we eventually did. With Goffredo, my production manager, I went to the nearest office of the Banco di Sicilia. I had to leave my briefcase outside the main entrance that was guarded by a machine gun-carrying official but was eventually able to telex the money to a numbered account in Palermo.   Returning to the hotel, there was a very obvious police presence outside and, being only too aware that what I had done was illegal, I headed straight for the airport.

The money duly arrived back minus the usual transfer fee.

Over the years, I received many compliments from agencies, clients and even competitors, but when I had a subsequent meeting with Karel, he paid me the greatest compliment which meant so much more coming from such an accomplished professional director. I cannot remember if Karel had chosen the cameraman, but I suspect not. I had put together the crew and he told me that it had been one of the best crews he had ever worked with.

In 1992, Jim decided that I was too old – and probably too expensive – for the image of the company he wanted to portray. I was being made redundant, but I had signed a contract for two Mars commercials, one with the English football squad and one with the award-winning relay team for the forthcoming Summer Olympics in Barcelona. He had fired me between the two shoots and had to keep me on until I had completed the Barcelona shoot and earned my bonus.

9

SPOT OF RAIN

Redundancy was to present me with new challenges and it was not very long before I was approached by my old client, Procter & Gamble, who had set up a direct purchasing scheme in an effort to control escalating costs. I was offered the job of supervising the companies who were employed to provide services on all P&G productions, art direction, studio hire, electrical and camera equipment and insurance.

I set up a partnership with Shirley and we began trading very quickly. I was given the responsibility for checking budgets submitted by agencies for their commercials. In other words, I became their cost consultant. I worked on all brands with the head office in Newcastle and the Egham office that handled cosmetic and other products ranging from Always to Max Factor. There were four major agencies handling P&G brands, Saatchi & Saatchi, Leo Burnett, Grey, and DMB&B, and my role frequently involved attending production meetings with all of them.

At first I was prepared to take on almost anything, and there are several entries for sales of picture framing to various friends. Very soon the P&G contract took over my time but there were some quite extraordinary events over the next few years. Becoming a consultant was, in fact, a completely logical development in view of my history and experience over many years. I still had a very high profile in the industry and with my established credit record would continue to have no difficulty if I wanted to produce on my own again, which in time I in fact did.

As already stated, Jim had made me redundant in the middle of a contract for two Mars commercials, so I found myself invoicing his company for my commission on the contract which was not completed until I was no longer an employee. In the first two months I worked on Clearasil, Biactol, Head & Shoulders, Fairy, Bold, Crest, Daz, Olay, Flash, Always, Ariel, and Pampers, earning a fee for each and frequently attending the production meetings with the relevant production company. Lenor and Viakal were soon added to the list, as was Old Spice and Pantene. Work on these brands would continue unabated, but soon I was being asked to take on other projects.

I had a call one day from a P&G executive who I had known many years earlier and he was asking me if I could produce a commercial for a brand that had not been released in the UK.

We met at a hotel in Leicester Square and he briefed me on the project. I was put in touch with a creative team working in Germany. I was given a budget and sourced a director who I felt would be best for the job and persuaded him to work for me through his own company. The project was successful in market tests and led to my being asked to produce more commercials for the product launch in the UK. I used another company owned by a friend and set up a shoot in Spain. As it involved children, I had to attend Westminster Magistrates' Court and undertake to ensure that the children only worked according to the laid down rules. It was a very bizarre situation, P&G were using me as an agency as they had not yet appointed one. I could and did get the commercial ready for transmission but could not, of course, book the actual transmission with the TV stations. At this point Saatchi & Saatchi was appointed and my role in that particular commercial was at an end. The brand was Sunny Delight. It was to have a successful launch but was relatively short lived due to serious health concerns.

Later I was asked to produce several commercials for Pampers with Saatchi & Saatchi, an agency that I had a very strong relationship with. Some time later I was asked to produce a series of commercials for Always, so in effect here I was running my own production company again, only this time from our spare bedroom in Sussex.

P&G continued to add new brands and eventually I found myself as a cost consultant looking at the budget for a major shoot for Max Factor with Madonna. I was occasionally to disagree with the creative director of the agency, a very determined lady, but she had relatives in the next village to us in Sussex and we always remained on good terms.

During this period I was called upon in my consultant capacity to attend conferences in Brussels, Istanbul and North Africa. I also became the company's representative on the industry negotiating body and was so listed in the official guide to production contracts. Quite apart from dealing with the four agencies, I also had responsibility for the suppliers that had been signed up to provide services on a contractual basis. Art direction and set construction was initially through a company known as BBRK, run by an art director David Bill. Unfortunately having taken over Ealing Studios, the company had taken on too much and they failed during one of the productions I was involved in. The construction crew were not going to be paid so I had little option but to step in, which I did, paying all and billing the cost back to P&G. Camera equipment was provided by ARRI Media and lighting was the responsibility of Samuelson lighting run by Michael Samuelson, the son of Sydney who had founded the business. That left the studio and the contract was with Magic Eye Studio in South London. Magic Eye had been set up by a photographer and his agent, Ian Dent Davis, who sadly was to die of lung cancer. I had visited him at his home and in the hospital two days before he died. I was shocked that no other business associate had the courage to do so.

It was now that yet another bizarre thing happened. Our younger daughter Jane and her partner went to dinner one evening in a pub not far from where we were living. This was not something that they had ever done before and over dinner another guest came over to her and said, "You're Geoff's daughter, aren't you?" It turned out to be an ex-art director from Saatchi & Saatchi with whom I had worked on many occasions and he asked Jane to get me to contact him. It turned out that he was the creative director of a small agency based in Maidstone and was looking for someone to produce a commercial for their client, P&O Ferries. It seems hard to believe that yet another door had opened just as one had closed, but it happened and I made a number of commercials for them, culminating in celebrating the introduction of two new ships on the Dover—Calais route.

At the same time as I was committed to this production, I had a call from Robert Amram in Mexico who had a project to advertise a well-known Mexican beer and they wanted to film in Europe. Not just in Europe but in Moscow and it was to feature the Red Army or a small contingent who were to be seen marching along and reacting to the product. I do not recall the script in detail as I did not attend the filming but I did set it up using my local contacts through P&G. I had too much work to be able to go to Moscow but was very happy with the fee I was paid for organizing it.

I soon had another approach, this time from the producer that I had made the Gilbey's and J&B commercials for. He had a creative director friend and had been directing commercials through an existing production company. He realized that if we got together we could do a lot better, so I added yet another string to my bow and we made several commercials for various brands including Uncle Ben's and several Mars brands. The best was yet to come and was another project for Russia, but this time it was to be filmed here in the UK. It was for a cigarette brand, Sovereign, and it was based on a gambler having backed a horse by that name which won the race. We filmed for two days at Kempton

Park and I was able to use my own video camera to superimpose the name over a shot of the horse on the screen above the bookies window.

It was a very successful exercise and our Russian clients went home well satisfied.

The company decided to restrict the number of production companies handling their work and this was to lead to the extraordinary situation where no agency could commission any production without my approval. I was not even an employee and yet I had enormous power over four of the biggest advertising agencies in London. Eventually, of course, it was to come to an end and it came about when having transferred a large volume of business to their European office in Brussels and discovering that it was not a very clever tax move, the brand management was transferred to Switzerland. It had become difficult to justify my retainer and the system became irrelevant.

By now I was approaching my 75th birthday and was ready to retire. Or was it that the industry had changed so much that I was becoming something of an anachronism?

During my fifty years in the business I enjoyed enormous luck, although looking back to my time with Pearl & Dean, I remember in one conversation with the chairman when Ernie said to me, "You make your own luck." Maybe hard work and integrity in an industry where so often it was not the norm had something to do with it, but that cannot account for the fact that

I always had good weather, or if I needed bad weather to trigger an insurance claim, I got it. And never lost a single penny due to inclement weather.

It's like I said, it never rains unless I want it to.

And...cut. Check the gate. That's a wrap, everyone. Ciao!

POSTSCRIPT

This book affords readers the opportunity to delve into the fascinating life of Geoffrey Forster, one of Britain's most famed TV commercial producers.

As a parting gesture, we thought it might be enlightening to hear what someone else – one of Geoff's old agency clients and a lifelong friend – remembers about working with Geoff in his heyday.

"I worked with Geoff in the 1970s, when I was the Creative Director at a now-defunct London agency. Newly arrived from Canada, I didn't know the first thing about producing. Not a clue. The only thing I knew was that I needed to launch a new car on television and in cinemas.

I talked to a ton of production companies in town, but felt they were all tired old toadies more interested in making a buck – or rather a quid – than a great commercial.

But from the moment I first met Geoff, he was a very different kettle of fish. No slick Willie or swaggering braggadocio, just a quiet, warm human being with an embarrassing abundance of diverse talents.

Apart from his starring role as a commercials producer, he was a past master of myriad talents including furniture making, embroidery, plumbing, even wine connoisseurship.

No matter what he turned his hand to, he always did it exceedingly well.

After I left London, I worked for agencies in Paris, Brussels, Lagos, Sydney, Auckland and finally Toronto. But in not one of these far-flung places did I manage to find anyone who came even remotely close to Geoffrey in terms of sheer talent, human decency, and the indomitable drive to be the best at bloody well everything he did."

D. Richard Truman

CPSIA information can be obtained
at www.ICGtesting.com
Printed in the USA
LVHW090409300421
686063LV00005B/48